Life Application Bible Studies
GALATIANS & EPHESIANS

APPLICATION® BIBLE STUDIES

galatians & ephesians

Part 1:
Complete text of Galatians and Ephesians with study notes
and features from the *Life Application Study Bible*

Part 2:
Thirteen lessons for individual or group study

Study questions written and edited by

Peter O'Donnell
Dr. James C. Galvin
Rev. David R. Veerman
Dr. Bruce B. Barton

New Living
Translation

Tyndale House Publishers, Inc.
Carol Stream, Illinois

Visit Tyndale's exciting Web sites at www.newlivingtranslation.com and www.tyndale.com.

New Living Translation, NLT, the New Living Translation logo, and *Life Application* are registered trademarks of Tyndale House Publishers, Inc.

Life Application Bible Studies: Galatians & Ephesians

Copyright © 1998, 2009 by Tyndale House Publishers, Inc., Carol Stream, Illinois 60188. All rights reserved.

Life Application notes and features copyright © 1988, 1989, 1990, 1991, 1993, 1996, 2004 by Tyndale House Publishers, Inc., Carol Stream, Illinois 60188. Maps in text copyright © 1986, 1988 by Tyndale House Publishers, Inc. All rights reserved.

Cover photograph copyright © by Steve Kitching/iStockphoto. All rights reserved.

The text of Galatians & Ephesians is from the *Holy Bible,* New Living Translation, copyright © 1996, 2004, 2007 by Tyndale House Foundation. All rights reserved.

ISBN 978-1-4143-2644-3

Printed in the United States of America

15   14   13
7   6   5   4   3

CONTENTS

A NOTE TO READERS

The *Holy Bible*, New Living Translation, was first published in 1996. It quickly became one of the most popular Bible translations in the English-speaking world. While the NLT's influence was rapidly growing, the Bible Translation Committee determined that an additional investment in scholarly review and text refinement could make it even better. So shortly after its initial publication, the committee began an eight-year process with the purpose of increasing the level of the NLT's precision without sacrificing its easy-to-understand quality. This second-generation text was completed in 2004 and is reflected in this edition of the New Living Translation. An additional update with minor changes was subsequently introduced in 2007.

The goal of any Bible translation is to convey the meaning and content of the ancient Hebrew, Aramaic, and Greek texts as accurately as possible to contemporary readers. The challenge for our translators was to create a text that would communicate as clearly and powerfully to today's readers as the original texts did to readers and listeners in the ancient biblical world. The resulting translation is easy to read and understand, while also accurately communicating the meaning and content of the original biblical texts. The NLT is a general-purpose text especially good for study, devotional reading, and reading aloud in worship services.

We believe that the New Living Translation—which combines the latest biblical scholarship with a clear, dynamic writing style—will communicate God's word powerfully to all who read it. We publish it with the prayer that God will use it to speak his timeless truth to the church and the world in a fresh, new way.

The Publishers
October 2007

INTRODUCTION TO THE NEW LIVING TRANSLATION

Translation Philosophy and Methodology

English Bible translations tend to be governed by one of two general translation theories. The first theory has been called "formal-equivalence," "literal," or "word-for-word" translation. According to this theory, the translator attempts to render each word of the original language into English and seeks to preserve the original syntax and sentence structure as much as possible in translation. The second theory has been called "dynamic-equivalence," "functional-equivalence," or "thought-for-thought" translation. The goal of this translation theory is to produce in English the closest natural equivalent of the message expressed by the original-language text, both in meaning and in style.

Both of these translation theories have their strengths. A formal-equivalence translation preserves aspects of the original text—including ancient idioms, term consistency, and original-language syntax—that are valuable for scholars and professional study. It allows a reader to trace formal elements of the original-language text through the English translation. A dynamic-equivalence translation, on the other hand, focuses on translating the message of the original-language text. It ensures that the meaning of the text is readily apparent to the contemporary reader. This allows the message to come through with immediacy, without requiring the reader to struggle with foreign idioms and awkward syntax. It also facilitates serious study of the text's message and clarity in both devotional and public reading.

The pure application of either of these translation philosophies would create translations at opposite ends of the translation spectrum. But in reality, all translations contain a mixture of these two philosophies. A purely formal-equivalence translation would be unintelligible in English, and a purely dynamic-equivalence translation would risk being unfaithful to the original. That is why translations shaped by dynamic-equivalence theory are usually quite literal when the original text is relatively clear, and the translations shaped by formal-equivalence theory are sometimes quite dynamic when the original text is obscure.

The translators of the New Living Translation set out to render the message of the original texts of Scripture into clear, contemporary English. As they did so, they kept the concerns of both formal-equivalence and dynamic-equivalence in mind. On the one hand, they translated as simply and literally as possible when that approach yielded an accurate, clear, and natural English text. Many words and phrases were rendered literally and consistently into English, preserving essential literary and rhetorical devices, ancient metaphors, and word choices that give structure to the text and provide echoes of meaning from one passage to the next.

On the other hand, the translators rendered the message more dynamically when the literal rendering was hard to understand, was misleading, or yielded archaic or foreign wording. They clarified difficult metaphors and terms to aid in the reader's understanding. The translators first struggled with the meaning of the words and phrases in the ancient context; then they rendered the message into clear, natural English. Their goal was to be both faithful to the ancient texts and eminently readable. The result is a translation that is both exegetically accurate and idiomatically powerful.

Translation Process and Team

To produce an accurate translation of the Bible into contemporary English, the translation team needed the skills necessary to enter into the thought patterns of the ancient authors and then to render their ideas, connotations, and effects into clear, contemporary English.

To begin this process, qualified biblical scholars were needed to interpret the meaning of the original text and to check it against our base English translation. In order to guard against personal and theological biases, the scholars needed to represent a diverse group of evangelicals who would employ the best exegetical tools. Then to work alongside the scholars, skilled English stylists were needed to shape the text into clear, contemporary English.

With these concerns in mind, the Bible Translation Committee recruited teams of scholars that represented a broad spectrum of denominations, theological perspectives, and backgrounds within the worldwide evangelical community. Each book of the Bible was assigned to three different scholars with proven expertise in the book or group of books to be reviewed. Each of these scholars made a thorough review of a base translation and submitted suggested revisions to the appropriate Senior Translator. The Senior Translator then reviewed and summarized these suggestions and proposed a first-draft revision of the base text. This draft served as the basis for several additional phases of exegetical and stylistic committee review. Then the Bible Translation Committee jointly reviewed and approved every verse of the final translation.

Throughout the translation and editing process, the Senior Translators and their scholar teams were given a chance to review the editing done by the team of stylists. This ensured that exegetical errors would not be introduced late in the process and that the entire Bible Translation Committee was happy with the final result. By choosing a team of qualified scholars and skilled stylists and by setting up a process that allowed their interaction throughout the process, the New Living Translation has been refined to preserve the essential formal elements of the original biblical texts, while also creating a clear, understandable English text.

The New Living Translation was first published in 1996. Shortly after its initial publication, the Bible Translation Committee began a process of further committee review and translation refinement. The purpose of this continued revision was to increase the level of precision without sacrificing the text's easy-to-understand quality. This second-edition text was completed in 2004, and an additional update with minor changes was subsequently introduced in 2007. This printing of the New Living Translation reflects the updated 2007 text.

Written to Be Read Aloud

It is evident in Scripture that the biblical documents were written to be read aloud, often in public worship (see Nehemiah 8; Luke 4:16-20; 1 Timothy 4:13; Revelation 1:3). It is still the case today that more people will hear the Bible read aloud in church than are likely to read it for themselves. Therefore, a new translation must communicate with clarity and power when it is read publicly. Clarity was a primary goal for the NLT translators, not only to facilitate private reading and understanding, but also to ensure that it would be excellent for public reading and make an immediate and powerful impact on any listener.

The Texts behind the New Living Translation

The Old Testament translators used the Masoretic Text of the Hebrew Bible as represented in *Biblia Hebraica Stuttgartensia* (1977), with its extensive system of textual notes; this is an update of Rudolf Kittel's *Biblia Hebraica* (Stuttgart, 1937). The translators also further compared the Dead Sea Scrolls, the Septuagint and other Greek manuscripts, the Samaritan Pentateuch, the Syriac Peshitta, the Latin Vulgate, and any other versions or manuscripts that shed light on the meaning of difficult passages.

The New Testament translators used the two standard editions of the Greek New Testament: the *Greek New Testament*, published by the United Bible Societies (UBS, fourth revised edition, 1993), and *Novum Testamentum Graece*, edited by Nestle and Aland (NA, twenty-seventh edition, 1993). These two editions, which have the same text but differ in punctuation and textual notes, represent, for the most part, the best in modern textual scholarship. However, in cases where strong textual or other scholarly evidence supported the decision, the translators sometimes chose to differ from the UBS and NA Greek texts and followed variant readings found in other ancient witnesses. Significant textual variants of this sort are always noted in the textual notes of the New Living Translation.

Translation Issues

The translators have made a conscious effort to provide a text that can be easily understood by the typical reader of modern English. To this end, we sought to use only vocabulary and language structures in common use today. We avoided using language likely to become quickly dated or that reflects only a narrow subdialect of English, with the goal of making the New Living Translation as broadly useful and timeless as possible.

But our concern for readability goes beyond the concerns of vocabulary and sentence structure. We are also concerned about historical and cultural barriers to understanding the Bible, and we have sought to translate terms shrouded in history and culture in ways that can be immediately understood. To this end:

- We have converted ancient weights and measures (for example, "ephah" [a unit of dry volume] or "cubit" [a unit of length]) to modern English (American) equivalents, since the ancient measures are not generally meaningful to today's readers. Then in the textual footnotes we offer the literal Hebrew, Aramaic, or Greek measures, along with modern metric equivalents.

- Instead of translating ancient currency values literally, we have expressed them in common terms that communicate the message. For example, in the Old Testament, "ten shekels of silver" becomes "ten pieces of silver" to convey the intended message. In the New Testament, we have often translated the "denarius" as "the normal daily wage" to facilitate understanding. Then a footnote offers: "Greek *a denarius*, the payment for a full day's wage." In general, we give a clear English rendering and then state the literal Hebrew, Aramaic, or Greek in a textual footnote.

- Since the names of Hebrew months are unknown to most contemporary readers, and since the Hebrew lunar calendar fluctuates from year to year in relation to the solar calendar used today, we have looked for clear ways to communicate the time of year the Hebrew months (such as Abib) refer to. When an expanded or interpretive rendering is given in the text, a textual note gives the literal rendering. Where it is possible to define a specific ancient date in terms of our modern calendar, we use modern dates in the text. A textual footnote then gives the literal Hebrew date and states the rationale for our rendering. For example, Ezra 6:15 pinpoints the date when the postexilic Temple was completed in Jerusalem: "the third day of the month Adar." This was during the sixth year of King Darius's reign (that is, 515 B.C.). We have translated that date as March 12, with a footnote giving the Hebrew and identifying the year as 515 B.C.

- Since ancient references to the time of day differ from our modern methods of denoting time, we have used renderings that are instantly understandable to the modern reader. Accordingly, we have rendered specific times of day by using approx-imate equivalents in terms of our common "o'clock" system. On occasion, transla-tions such as "at dawn the next morning" or "as the sun was setting" have been used when the biblical reference is more general.

- When the meaning of a proper name (or a wordplay inherent in a proper name) is relevant to the message of the text, its meaning is often illuminated with a textual footnote. For example, in Exodus 2:10 the text reads: "The princess named him Moses, for she explained, 'I lifted him out of the water.'" The accompanying footnote reads: "*Moses* sounds like a Hebrew term that means 'to lift out.'"

  Sometimes, when the actual meaning of a name is clear, that meaning is included in parentheses within the text itself. For example, the text at Genesis 16:11 reads: "You are to name him Ishmael *(which means 'God hears')*, for the Lord has heard your cry of distress." Since the original hearers and readers would have instantly understood the meaning of the name "Ishmael," we have provided modern readers with the same information so they can experience the text in a similar way.

- Many words and phrases carry a great deal of cultural meaning that was obvious to the original readers but needs explanation in our own culture. For example, the phrase "they beat their breasts" (Luke 23:48) in ancient times meant that people were very upset, often in mourning. In our translation we chose to translate this phrase dynamically for clarity: "They went home *in deep sorrow*." Then we included a footnote with the literal Greek, which reads: "Greek *went home beating their breasts*." In other similar cases, however, we have sometimes chosen to illuminate the existing literal expression to make it immediately understandable. For example, here we might have expanded the literal Greek phrase to read: "They went home beating their breasts *in sorrow."* If we had done this, we would not have included a textual footnote, since the literal Greek clearly appears in translation.

- Metaphorical language is sometimes difficult for contemporary readers to understand, so at times we have chosen to translate or illuminate the meaning of a metaphor. For example, the ancient poet writes, "Your neck is *like* the tower of David" (Song of Songs 4:4). We have rendered it "Your neck is *as beautiful as* the tower of David" to clarify the intended positive meaning of the simile. Another example comes in Ecclesiastes 12:3, which can be literally rendered: "Remember him . . . when the grinding women cease because they are few, and the women who look through the windows see dimly." We have rendered it: "Remember him before your teeth—your few remaining servants—stop grinding; and before your eyes—the women looking through the windows—see dimly." We clarified such metaphors only when we believed a typical reader might be confused by the literal text.

- When the content of the original language text is poetic in character, we have rendered it in English poetic form. We sought to break lines in ways that clarify and highlight the relationships between phrases of the text. Hebrew poetry often uses parallelism, a literary form where a second phrase (or in some instances a third or fourth) echoes the initial phrase in some way. In Hebrew parallelism, the subsequent parallel phrases continue, while also furthering and sharpening, the thought expressed in the initial line or phrase. Whenever possible, we sought to represent these parallel phrases in natural poetic English.

- The Greek term *hoi Ioudaioi* is literally translated "the Jews" in many English translations. In the Gospel of John, however, this term doesn't always refer to the Jewish people generally. In some contexts, it refers more particularly to the Jewish religious leaders. We have attempted to capture the meaning in these different contexts by using terms such as "the people" (with a footnote: Greek *the Jewish people*) or "the religious leaders," where appropriate.

- One challenge we faced was how to translate accurately the ancient biblical text that was originally written in a context where male-oriented terms were used to refer to humanity generally. We needed to respect the nature of the ancient context while also trying to make the translation clear to a modern audience that tends to read male-oriented language as applying only to males. Often the original text, though using masculine nouns and pronouns, clearly intends that the message be applied to both men and women. A typical example is found in the New Testament letters, where the believers are called "brothers" (*adelphoi*). Yet it is clear from the content of these letters that they were addressed to all the believers—male and female. Thus, we have usually translated this Greek word as "brothers and sisters" in order to represent the historical situation more accurately.

  We have also been sensitive to passages where the text applies generally to human beings or to the human condition. In some instances we have used plural pronouns (they, them) in place of the masculine singular (he, him). For example, a traditional rendering of Proverbs 22:6 is: "Train up a child in the way he should go, and when he is old he will not turn from it." We have rendered it: "Direct your children onto the right path, and when they are older, they will not leave it." At times, we have also replaced third person pronouns with the second person to ensure clarity. A traditional rendering of Proverbs 26:27 is: "He who digs a pit will fall into it, and he who rolls a stone, it will come back on him." We have rendered it: "If you set a trap for others, you will get caught in it yourself. If you roll a boulder down on others, it will crush you instead."

  We should emphasize, however, that all masculine nouns and pronouns used to represent God (for example, "Father") have been maintained without exception. All decisions of this kind have been driven by the concern to reflect accurately the intended meaning of the original texts of Scripture.

Lexical Consistency in Terminology
For the sake of clarity, we have translated certain original-language terms consistently, especially within synoptic passages and for commonly repeated rhetorical phrases, and within

certain word categories such as divine names and non-theological technical terminology (e.g., liturgical, legal, cultural, zoological, and botanical terms). For theological terms, we have allowed a greater semantic range of acceptable English words or phrases for a single Hebrew or Greek word. We have avoided some theological terms that are not readily understood by many modern readers. For example, we avoided using words such as "justification" and "sanctification," which are carryovers from Latin translations. In place of these words, we have provided renderings such as "made right with God" and "made holy."

The Spelling of Proper Names

Many individuals in the Bible, especially the Old Testament, are known by more than one name (e.g., Uzziah/Azariah). For the sake of clarity, we have tried to use a single spelling for any one individual, footnoting the literal spelling whenever we differ from it. This is especially helpful in delineating the kings of Israel and Judah. King Joash/Jehoash of Israel has been consistently called Jehoash, while King Joash/Jehoash of Judah is called Joash. A similar distinction has been used to distinguish between Joram/Jehoram of Israel and Joram/Jehoram of Judah. All such decisions were made with the goal of clarifying the text for the reader. When the ancient biblical writers clearly had a theological purpose in their choice of a variant name (e.g., Esh-baal/Ishbosheth), the different names have been maintained with an explanatory footnote.

For the names Jacob and Israel, which are used interchangeably for both the individual patriarch and the nation, we generally render it "Israel" when it refers to the nation and "Jacob" when it refers to the individual. When our rendering of the name differs from the underlying Hebrew text, we provide a textual footnote, which includes this explanation: "The names 'Jacob' and 'Israel' are often interchanged throughout the Old Testament, referring sometimes to the individual patriarch and sometimes to the nation."

The Rendering of Divine Names

All appearances of *'el, 'elohim,* or *'eloah* have been translated "God," except where the context demands the translation "god(s)." We have generally rendered the tetragrammaton (*YHWH*) consistently as "the LORD," utilizing a form with small capitals that is common among English translations. This will distinguish it from the name *'adonai,* which we render "Lord." When *'adonai* and *YHWH* appear together, we have rendered it "Sovereign LORD." This also distinguishes *'adonai YHWH* from cases where *YHWH* appears with *'elohim,* which is rendered "LORD God." When *YH* (the short form of *YHWH*) and *YHWH* appear together, we have rendered it "LORD GOD." When *YHWH* appears with the term *tseba'oth,* we have rendered it "LORD of Heaven's Armies" to translate the meaning of the name. In a few cases, we have utilized the transliteration, *Yahweh,* when the personal character of the name is being invoked in contrast to another divine name or the name of some other god (for example, see Exodus 3:15; 6:2-3).

In the New Testament, the Greek word *christos* has been translated as "Messiah" when the context assumes a Jewish audience. When a Gentile audience can be assumed, *christos* has been translated as "Christ." The Greek word *kurios* is consistently translated "Lord," except that it is translated "LORD" wherever the New Testament text explicitly quotes from the Old Testament, and the text there has it in small capitals.

Textual Footnotes

The New Living Translation provides several kinds of textual footnotes, all designated in the text with an asterisk:

- When for the sake of clarity the NLT renders a difficult or potentially confusing phrase dynamically, we generally give the literal rendering in a textual footnote. This allows the reader to see the literal source of our dynamic rendering and how our translation relates to other more literal translations. These notes are prefaced with "Hebrew," "Aramaic," or "Greek," identifying the language of the underlying source text. For example, in Acts 2:42 we translated the literal "breaking of bread" (from the Greek) as "the Lord's Supper" to clarify that this verse refers to the ceremonial practice of the church rather than just an ordinary meal. Then we attached a footnote to "the Lord's Supper," which reads: "Greek *the breaking of bread.*"

- Textual footnotes are also used to show alternative renderings, prefaced with the word "Or." These normally occur for passages where an aspect of the meaning is debated. On occasion, we also provide notes on words or phrases that represent a departure from long-standing tradition. These notes are prefaced with "Tradition-ally rendered." For example, the footnote to the translation "serious skin disease" at Leviticus 13:2 says: "Traditionally rendered *leprosy.* The Hebrew word used throughout this passage is used to describe various skin diseases."
- When our translators follow a textual variant that differs significantly from our stan-dard Hebrew or Greek texts (listed earlier), we document that difference with a foot-note. We also footnote cases when the NLT excludes a passage that is included in the Greek text known as the *Textus Receptus* (and familiar to readers through its transla-tion in the King James Version). In such cases, we offer a translation of the excluded text in a footnote, even though it is generally recognized as a later addition to the Greek text and not part of the original Greek New Testament.
- All Old Testament passages that are quoted in the New Testament are identified by a textual footnote at the New Testament location. When the New Testament clearly quotes from the Greek translation of the Old Testament, and when it differs signifi-cantly in wording from the Hebrew text, we also place a textual footnote at the Old Testament location. This note includes a rendering of the Greek version, along with a cross-reference to the New Testament passage(s) where it is cited (for example, see notes on Proverbs 3:12; Psalms 8:2; 53:3).
- Some textual footnotes provide cultural and historical information on places, things, and people in the Bible that are probably obscure to modern readers. Such notes should aid the reader in understanding the message of the text. For example, in Acts 12:1, "King Herod" is named in this translation as "King Herod Agrippa" and is iden-tified in a footnote as being "the nephew of Herod Antipas and a grandson of Herod the Great."
- When the meaning of a proper name (or a wordplay inherent in a proper name) is relevant to the meaning of the text, it is either illuminated with a textual footnote or included within parentheses in the text itself. For example, the footnote concerning the name "Eve" at Genesis 3:20 reads: "*Eve* sounds like a Hebrew term that means 'to give life.' " This wordplay in the Hebrew illuminates the meaning of the text, which goes on to say that Eve "would be the mother of all who live."

As WE SUBMIT this translation for publication, we recognize that any translation of the Scrip-tures is subject to limitations and imperfections. Anyone who has attempted to communi-cate the richness of God's Word into another language will realize it is impossible to make a perfect translation. Recognizing these limitations, we sought God's guidance and wisdom throughout this project. Now we pray that he will accept our efforts and use this translation for the benefit of the church and of all people.

We pray that the New Living Translation will overcome some of the barriers of history, cul-ture, and language that have kept people from reading and understanding God's Word. We hope that readers unfamiliar with the Bible will find the words clear and easy to understand and that readers well versed in the Scriptures will gain a fresh perspective. We pray that readers will gain insight and wisdom for living, but most of all that they will meet the God of the Bible and be forever changed by knowing him.

The Bible Translation Committee
October 2007

WHY THE
LIFE APPLICATION STUDY BIBLE
IS UNIQUE

Have you ever opened your Bible and asked the following:

- What does this passage really mean?
- How does it apply to my life?
- Why does some of the Bible seem irrelevant?
- What do these ancient cultures have to do with today?
- I love God; why can't I understand what he is saying to me through his word?
- What's going on in the lives of these Bible people?

Many Christians do not read the Bible regularly. Why? Because in the pressures of daily living they cannot find a connection between the timeless principles of Scripture and the ever-present problems of day-by-day living.

God urges us to apply his word (Isaiah 42:23; 1 Corinthians 10:11; 2 Thessalonians 3:4), but too often we stop at accumulating Bible knowledge. This is why the *Life Application Study Bible* was developed—to show how to put into practice what we have learned.

Applying God's word is a vital part of one's relationship with God; it is the evidence that we are obeying him. The difficulty in applying the Bible is not with the Bible itself, but with the reader's inability to bridge the gap between the past and present, the conceptual and practical. When we don't or can't do this, spiritual dryness, shallowness, and indifference are the results.

The words of Scripture itself cry out to us, "But don't just listen to God's word. You must do what it says. Otherwise, you are only fooling yourselves" (James 1:22). The *Life Application Study Bible* helps us to obey God's word. Developed by an interdenominational team of pastors, scholars, family counselors, and a national organization dedicated to promoting God's word and spreading the gospel, the *Life Application Study Bible* took many years to complete. All the work was reviewed by several renowned theologians under the directorship of Dr. Kenneth Kantzer.

The *Life Application Study Bible* does what a good resource Bible should: It helps you understand the context of a passage, gives important background and historical information, explains difficult words and phrases, and helps you see the interrelationship of Scripture. But it does much more. The *Life Application Study Bible* goes deeper into God's word, helping you discover the timeless truth being communicated, see the relevance for your life, and make a personal application. While some study Bibles attempt application, over 75 percent of this Bible is application oriented. The notes answer the questions "So what?" and "What does this passage mean to me, my family, my friends, my job, my neighborhood, my church, my country?"

Imagine reading a familiar passage of Scripture and gaining fresh insight, as if it were the first time you had ever read it. How much richer your life would be if you left each Bible reading with a new perspective and a small change for the better. A small change every day adds up to a changed life—and that is the very purpose of Scripture.

WHAT IS APPLICATION?

The best way to define application is to first determine what it is *not*. Application is *not* just accumulating knowledge. Accumulating knowledge helps us discover and understand facts and concepts, but it stops there. History is filled with philosophers who knew what the Bible said but failed to apply it to their lives, keeping them from believing and changing. Many think that understanding is the end goal of Bible study, but it is really only the beginning.

Application is *not* just illustration. Illustration only tells us how someone else handled a similar situation. While we may empathize with that person, we still have little direction for our personal situation.

Application is *not* just making a passage "relevant." Making the Bible relevant only helps us to see that the same lessons that were true in Bible times are true today; it does not show us how to apply them to the problems and pressures of our individual lives.

What, then, is application? Application begins by knowing and understanding God's word and its timeless truths. *But you cannot stop there.* If you do, God's word may not change your life, and it may become dull, difficult, tedious, and tiring. A good application focuses the truth of God's word, shows the reader what to do about what is being read, and motivates the reader to respond to what God is teaching. All three are essential to application.

Application is putting into practice what we already know (see Mark 4:24 and Hebrews 5:14) and answering the question "So what?" by confronting us with the right questions and motivating us to take action (see 1 John 2:5-6 and James 2:26). Application is deeply personal—unique for each individual. It makes a relevant truth a personal truth and involves developing a strategy and action plan to live your life in harmony with the Bible. It is the biblical "how to" of life.

You may ask, "How can your application notes be relevant to my life?" Each application note has three parts: (1) an *explanation*, which ties the note directly to the Scripture passage and sets up the truth that is being taught; (2) the *bridge*, which explains the timeless truth and makes it relevant for today; (3) the *application*, which shows you how to take the timeless truth and apply it to your personal situation. No note, by itself, can apply Scripture directly to your life. It can only teach, direct, lead, guide, inspire, recommend, and urge. It can give you the resources and direction you need to apply the Bible, but only you can take these resources and put them into practice.

A good note, therefore should not only give you knowledge and understanding but point you to application. Before you buy any kind of resource study Bible, you should evaluate the notes and ask the following questions: (1) Does the note contain enough information to help me understand the point of the Scripture passage? (2) Does the note assume I know more than I do? (3) Does the note avoid denominational bias? (4) Do the notes touch most of life's experiences? (5) Does the note help me apply God's word?

FEATURES OF THE
LIFE APPLICATION STUDY BIBLE

NOTES

In addition to providing the reader with many application notes, the *Life Application Study Bible* also offers several kinds of explanatory notes, which help the reader understand culture, history, context, difficult-to-understand passages, background, places, theological concepts, and the relationship of various passages in Scripture to other passages.

BOOK INTRODUCTIONS

Each book introduction is divided into several easy-to-find parts:

Timeline. A guide that puts the Bible book into its historical setting. It lists the key events and the dates when they occurred.

Vital Statistics. A list of straight facts about the book—those pieces of information you need to know at a glance.

Overview. A summary of the book with general lessons and applications that can be learned from the book as a whole.

Blueprint. The outline of the book. It is printed in easy-to-understand language and is designed for easy memorization. To the right of each main heading is a key lesson that is taught in that particular section.

Megathemes. A section that gives the main themes of the Bible book, explains their significance, and then tells you why they are still important for us today.

Map. If included, this shows the key places found in that book and retells the story of the book from a geographical point of view.

OUTLINE

The *Life Application Study Bible* has a new, custom-made outline that was designed specifically from an application point of view. Several unique features should be noted:

1. To avoid confusion and to aid memory work, the book outline has only three levels for headings. Main outline heads are marked with a capital letter. Subheads are marked by a number. Minor explanatory heads have no letter or number.

2. Each main outline head marked by a letter also has a brief paragraph below it summarizing the Bible text and offering a general application.

3. Parallel passages are listed where they apply.

PERSONALITY PROFILES

Among the unique features of this Bible are the profiles of key Bible people, including their strengths and weaknesses, greatest accomplishments and mistakes, and key lessons from their lives.

MAPS

The *Life Application Study Bible* has a thorough and comprehensive Bible atlas built right into the book. There are two kinds of maps: a book-introduction map, telling the story of the book, and thumbnail maps in the notes, plotting most geographic movements.

CHARTS AND DIAGRAMS

Many charts and diagrams are included to help the reader better visualize difficult concepts or relationships. Most charts not only present the needed information but show the significance of the information as well.

CROSS-REFERENCES

An updated, exhaustive cross-reference system in the margins of the Bible text helps the reader find related passages quickly.

TEXTUAL NOTES

Directly related to the text of the New Living Translation, the textual notes provide explanations on certain wording in the translation, alternate translations, and information about readings in the ancient manuscripts.

HIGHLIGHTED NOTES

In each Bible study lesson, you will be asked to read specific notes as part of your preparation. These notes have each been highlighted by a bullet (•) so that you can find them easily.

GALATIANS

GALATIANS

VITAL STATISTICS

PURPOSE:
To refute the Judaizers (who taught that Gentile believers must obey the Jewish law in order to be saved), and to call Christians to faith and freedom in Christ

AUTHOR:
Paul

ORIGINAL AUDIENCE:
The churches in southern Galatia, founded on Paul's first missionary journey (including Iconium, Lystra, Derbe)

DATE WRITTEN:
Approximately A.D. 49, from Antioch, prior to the Jerusalem council (A.D. 50)

SETTING:
The most pressing controversy in the early church was the relationship of new believers, particularly Gentiles, to the Jewish laws. This was especially a problem for the converts and for the young churches that Paul had founded on his first missionary journey. Paul wrote to correct this problem. Later, at the council in Jerusalem, the conflict was officially resolved by the church leaders.

KEY VERSE:
"So Christ has truly set us free. Now make sure that you stay free, and don't get tied up again in slavery to the law" (5:1).

KEY PEOPLE:
Paul, Peter, Barnabas, Titus, Abraham, false teachers

KEY PLACES:
Galatia, Jerusalem

SPECIAL FEATURES:
This letter is not addressed to any specific body of believers and was probably circulated to several churches in Galatia.

A FAMILY, executing their carefully planned escape at midnight, dashing for the border . . . a man standing outside prison walls, gulping fresh air, awash in the new sun . . . a young woman with every trace of the ravaging drug gone from her system . . . they are FREE! With fresh anticipation, they can begin life anew.

Whether fleeing oppression, stepping out of prison, or breaking a strangling habit, freedom means life. There is nothing so exhilarating as knowing that the past is forgotten and that new options await. People yearn to be free.

The book of Galatians is the charter of Christian freedom. In this profound letter, Paul proclaims the reality of our liberty in Christ—freedom from the law and the power of sin, and freedom to serve our living Lord.

Most of the first converts and early leaders in the church were Jewish Christians who proclaimed Jesus as their Messiah. As Jewish Christians, they struggled with a dual identity: Their Jewishness constrained them to be strict followers of the law; their newfound faith in Christ invited them to celebrate a holy liberty. They wondered how Gentiles (non-Jews) could be part of the Kingdom of Heaven.

This controversy tore the early church. Judaizers—an extremist Jewish faction within the church—taught that Gentile Christians had to submit to Jewish laws and traditions *in addition to* believing in Christ. As a missionary to the Gentiles, Paul had to confront this issue many times.

Galatians was written, therefore, to refute the Judaizers and to call believers back to the pure gospel. The Good News is for all people—Jews and Gentiles alike. Salvation is by God's grace through faith in Christ Jesus *and nothing else*. Faith in Christ means true freedom.

After a brief introduction (1:1–5), Paul addresses those who were accepting the Judaizers' perverted gospel (1:6–9). He summarizes the controversy, including his personal confrontation with Peter and other church leaders (1:10—2:16). He then demonstrates that salvation is by faith alone by alluding to his conversion (2:17–21), appealing to his readers' own experience of the gospel (3:1–5), and showing how the Old Testament teaches about grace (3:6–20). Next, he explains the purpose of God's laws and the relationship between law, God's promises, and Christ (3:21—4:31).

Having laid the foundation, Paul builds his case for Christian liberty. We are saved by faith, not by keeping the law (5:1–12); our freedom means that we are free to love and serve one another, not to do wrong (5:13–26); and Christians should carry each other's burdens and be kind to each other (6:1–10). In 6:11–18, Paul takes the pen into his own hand and shares his final thoughts.

As you read Galatians, try to understand this first-century conflict between grace and law, or faith and deeds, but also be aware of modern parallels. Like Paul, defend the truth of the gospel and reject all those who would add to or twist this truth. You are *free* in Christ—step into the light and celebrate!

THE BLUEPRINT

1. Authenticity of the gospel
   (1:1—2:21)
2. Superiority of the gospel
   (3:1—4:31)
3. Freedom of the gospel
   (5:1—6:18)

In response to attacks from false teachers, Paul wrote to defend his apostleship and the authority of the gospel. The Galatians were beginning to turn from faith to legalism. The struggle between the gospel and legalism is still a relevant issue. Many today would have us return to trying to earn God's favor through following rituals or obeying a set of rules. As Christians, we are not boxed in but set free. To preserve our freedom, we must stay close to Christ and resist any who promote subtle ways for us to earn our salvation.

MEGATHEMES

THEME	EXPLANATION	IMPORTANCE
Law	A group of Jewish teachers insisted that non-Jewish believers must obey Jewish law and traditional rules. They believed a person was saved by following the law of Moses (with emphasis on circumcision, the sign of the covenant), in addition to faith in Christ. Paul opposed them by showing that the law can't save anyone.	We can't be saved by keeping the Old Testament law, even the Ten Commandments. The law served as a guide to point out our need to be forgiven. Christ fulfilled the obligations of the law for us. We must turn to him to be saved. He alone can make us right with God.
Faith	We are saved from God's judgment and penalty for sin by God's gracious gift to us. We receive salvation by faith—trusting in him—not in anything else. Becoming a Christian is in no way based on our initiative, wise choice, or good character. We can be right with God only by believing in him.	Your acceptance with God comes by believing in Christ alone. You must never add to or twist this truth. We are saved by faith, not by the good that we do. Have you placed your whole trust and confidence in Christ? He alone can forgive you and bring you into a relationship with God.
Freedom	Galatians is our charter of Christian freedom. We are not under the jurisdiction of Jewish laws and traditions nor under the authority of Jerusalem. Faith in Christ brings true freedom from sin and from the futile attempt to be right with God by keeping the law.	We are free in Christ, and yet freedom is a privilege. We are not free to disobey Christ or practice immorality, but we are free to serve the risen Christ. Let us use our freedom to love and to serve, not to do wrong.
Holy Spirit	We become Christians through the work of the Holy Spirit. He brings new life; even our faith to believe is a gift from him. The Holy Spirit instructs, guides, leads, and gives us power. He ends our bondage to evil desires, and he creates in us love, joy, peace, and many other wonderful changes.	When the Holy Spirit leads us, he produces his fruit in us. Just as we are saved by faith, not deeds, we also grow by faith. By believing, we can have the Holy Spirit within us, helping us live for Christ. Obey Christ by following the Holy Spirit's leading.

1. Authenticity of the gospel

Greetings from Paul

1:1
Acts 20:24

1 This letter is from Paul, an apostle. I was not appointed by any group of people or any human authority, but by Jesus Christ himself and by God the Father, who raised Jesus from the dead.

1:3
Rom 1:7
Phil 1:2
Phlm 1:3

2 All the brothers and sisters* here join me in sending this letter to the churches of Galatia.

3 May God our Father and the Lord Jesus Christ* give you grace and peace. 4 Jesus gave his life for our sins, just as God our Father planned, in order to rescue us from this evil world in which we live. 5 All glory to God forever and ever! Amen.

1:4
Rom 4:25
Gal 2:20
1 Tim 2:6
Titus 2:14
1:5
Rom 11:36

1:2 Greek *brothers;* also in 1:11.   **1:3** Some manuscripts read *God the Father and our Lord Jesus Christ.*

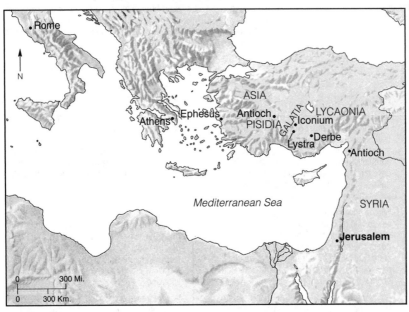

CITIES IN GALATIA
Paul visited several cities in Galatia on each of his three missionary journeys. On his first journey he went through Antioch in Pisidia, Iconium, Lystra, and Derbe, and then retraced his steps; on his second journey he went by land from Antioch of Syria through the four cities in Galatia; on his third journey he also went through those cities on the main route to Ephesus.

• **1:1** Paul and Barnabas had just completed their first missionary journey (Acts 13:2–14:28). They had visited Iconium, Lystra, and Derbe, cities in the Roman province of Galatia (present-day Turkey). Upon returning to Antioch, Paul was accused by some Jewish Christians of diluting Christianity to make it more appealing to Gentiles. These Jewish Christians disagreed with Paul's statements that Gentiles did not have to follow many of the religious laws that the Jews had obeyed for centuries. Some of Paul's accusers had even followed him to those Galatian cities and had told the Gentile converts they had to be circumcised and follow all the Jewish laws and customs in order to be saved. According to these people, Gentiles had to first become Jews in order to become Christians.

In response to this threat, Paul wrote this letter to the Galatian churches. In it, he explains that following the Old Testament laws, or the Jewish laws, will not bring salvation. A person is saved by grace through faith. Paul wrote this letter about A.D. 49, shortly before the meeting of the Jerusalem council, which settled the law-versus-grace controversy (Acts 15).

1:1 Paul explained his apostleship in these words, not to separate himself from the original Twelve, but to show that his apostleship rested on the same basis as theirs. If the believers in Galatia questioned Paul's apostleship, then they also should question the apostleship of Peter, John, James, and all the others—and such questioning would be absurd. All the apostles were called by Jesus Christ and God the Father, and they answered to God as their final authority.

1:1 For more information about Paul's life, see his Profile in Acts 9, p. 1837. Paul had been a Christian for about 15 years at this time.

• **1:2** In Paul's time, Galatia was the Roman province located in the center section of present-day Turkey. Much of the region rests on a large and fertile plateau, and large numbers of people had moved to the region because of its favorable agriculture. One of Paul's goals during his missionary journeys was to visit regions with large population centers in order to reach as many people as possible.

• **1:3-5** God's plan all along was to save us by Jesus' death. We have been rescued from the power of this present evil world— a world ruled by Satan and full of cruelty, tragedy, temptation, and deception. Being rescued from this evil world doesn't mean that we are taken out of it but that we are no longer enslaved to it. You were saved to live for God. Does your life reflect your gratitude for being rescued? Have you transferred your loyalty from this world to Christ?

There Is Only One Good News

1:6
2 Cor 11:4

1:7
Acts 15:1, 24
Gal 5:10

1:8
2 Cor 11:14

1:9
Deut 4:2; 12:32
1 Cor 16:22
Rev 22:18

⁶I am shocked that you are turning away so soon from God, who called you to himself through the loving mercy of Christ.* You are following a different way that pretends to be the Good News ⁷but is not the Good News at all. You are being fooled by those who deliberately twist the truth concerning Christ.

⁸Let God's curse fall on anyone, including us or even an angel from heaven, who preaches a different kind of Good News than the one we preached to you. ⁹I say again what we have said before: If anyone preaches any other Good News than the one you welcomed, let that person be cursed.

1:6 Some manuscripts read *through loving mercy.*

THE MARKS OF THE TRUE GOSPEL AND OF FALSE GOSPELS

Marks of a false gospel	Marks of the true gospel
2:21 . . . . Treats Christ's death as meaningless	1:11, 12 . . . . Teaches that the source of the gospel is God
3:12 . . . . Says people must obey the law in order to be saved	2:20 . . . . Knows that life is obtained through death; we trust in the Son of God who loved us and died for us so that we might die to sin and live for him
4:10 . . . . Tries to find favor with God by observing certain rituals	3:14 . . . . Explains that all believers have the Holy Spirit through faith
5:4 . . . . Counts on keeping laws to be right with God	3:21, 22 . . . . Declares that we cannot be saved by keeping laws; the only way of salvation is through faith in Christ, which is available to all
	3:26-28 . . . . Says that all believers are one in Christ, so there is no basis for discrimination of any kind
	5:24, 25 . . . . Proclaims that we are free from the grip of sin and that the Holy Spirit's power fills and guides us

---

• **1:6** Some people were preaching "a different way." They were teaching that to be saved, Gentile believers had to follow Jewish laws and customs, especially the rite of circumcision. Faith in Christ was not enough. This message undermined the truth that salvation is a gift, not a reward for certain deeds. Jesus Christ has made this gift available to all people, not just to Jews. Beware of people who say that we need more than simple faith in Christ to be saved. When people set up additional requirements for salvation, they deny the power of Christ's death on the cross (see 3:1-5).

• **1:7** The Bible says there is only one way to be forgiven of sin: by believing in Jesus Christ as Savior and Lord. No other person, method, or ritual can give eternal life. Attempting to be open-minded and tolerant, some people assert that all religions are equally valid paths to God. In a free society, people have the right to their religious opinions, but this doesn't guarantee that their ideas are right. God does not accept man-made religion as a substitute for faith in Jesus Christ. He has provided just one way—Jesus Christ (John 14:6).

1:7 Those who had confused the Galatian believers and perverted the Good News were zealous Jewish Christians who believed that the Old Testament practices, such as circumcision and dietary restrictions, were required of all believers. Because these teachers wanted to turn the Gentile Christians into Jews, they were called "Judaizers."

Most of the Galatian Christians were Greeks who were unfamiliar with Jewish laws and customs. The Judaizers were an extreme faction of Jewish Christians. Both groups believed in Christ, but their life-styles differed considerably. We do not know why the Judaizers may have traveled no small distance to teach their mistaken notions to the new Gentile converts. They may have been motivated by (1) a sincere wish to integrate Judaism with the new Christian faith, (2) a sincere love for their Jewish heritage, or (3) a jealous desire to destroy Paul's authority. Whether or not these Judaizers were sincere, their teaching threatened these new churches and had to be countered. When Paul said that their teaching twisted and changed the Good News, he was not rejecting everything Jewish. He himself was a Jew who worshiped in the Temple and attended the religious festivals. But he was concerned that *nothing* get in the way of the simple truth of his message— that salvation, for Jews and Gentiles alike, is through faith in Jesus Christ alone. Some time after the letter to the Galatians was sent, Paul met with the apostles in Jerusalem to discuss this matter further (see Acts 15).

• **1:7** A twisting of the truth is more difficult to spot than an outright lie. The Judaizers were twisting the truth about Christ. They claimed to follow him, but they denied that Jesus' work on the cross was sufficient for salvation. There will always be people who twist the Good News. Either they do not understand what the Bible teaches, or they are uncomfortable with the truth as it stands. How can we tell when people are twisting the truth? Before accepting the teachings of any group, find out what the group teaches about Jesus Christ. If their teaching does not match the truth in God's Word, then it is not true.

1:8, 9 Paul strongly denounced the Judaizers' twisting of the Good News. He said that God's curse should fall on anyone, even an angel from heaven, who came preaching a different kind of Good News. If an angel came preaching another message, he would not be from heaven, no matter how he looked. In 2 Corinthians 11:14, 15, Paul warned that Satan disguises himself as an angel of light. Here he invoked a curse on any angel who spreads a false teaching—a fitting response to an emissary of hell. Paul extended that curse to include himself if he should twist the Good News. His message must never change, for the truth of the Good News never changes. Paul used strong language because he was dealing with a life-and-death issue.

¹⁰Obviously, I'm not trying to win the approval of people, but of God. If pleasing people were my goal, I would not be Christ's servant.

1:10
1 Thes 2:4

Paul's Message Comes from Christ

¹¹Dear brothers and sisters, I want you to understand that the gospel message I preach is not based on mere human reasoning. ¹²I received my message from no human source, and no one taught me. Instead, I received it by direct revelation from Jesus Christ.*

1:12
1 Cor 2:10
Gal 1:1, 15-16
Eph 3:3

¹³You know what I was like when I followed the Jewish religion—how I violently persecuted God's church. I did my best to destroy it. ¹⁴I was far ahead of my fellow Jews in my zeal for the traditions of my ancestors.

1:13
Acts 8:3; 9:21;
22:4-5; 26:4-11

1:14
Acts 22:3

¹⁵But even before I was born, God chose me and called me by his marvelous grace. Then it pleased him ¹⁶to reveal his Son to me* so that I would proclaim the Good News about Jesus to the Gentiles.

When this happened, I did not rush out to consult with any human being.* ¹⁷Nor did I go up to Jerusalem to consult with those who were apostles before I was. Instead, I went away into Arabia, and later I returned to the city of Damascus.

1:15
Acts 9:15

1:16
Rom 1:17; 8:3, 10
Gal 2:9, 20
Col 1:27

¹⁸Then three years later I went to Jerusalem to get to know Peter,* and I stayed with him for fifteen days. ¹⁹The only other apostle I met at that time was James, the Lord's brother. ²⁰I declare before God that what I am writing to you is not a lie.

1:18
Acts 9:22-23, 26-27

1:19
Matt 13:55
Acts 15:13
Gal 2:9, 12

²¹After that visit I went north into the provinces of Syria and Cilicia. ²²And still the Christians in the churches in Judea didn't know me personally. ²³All they knew was that people were saying, "The one who used to persecute us is now preaching the very faith he tried to destroy!" ²⁴And they praised God because of me.

1:23
Acts 9:20

1:12 Or *by the revelation of Jesus Christ.*   **1:16a** Or *in me.*   **1:16b** Greek *with flesh and blood.*
1:18 Greek *Cephas.*

● **1:10** Do you spend your life trying to please everybody? Paul had to speak harshly to the Christians in Galatia because they were in serious danger. He did not apologize for his straightforward words, knowing that he could not serve Christ faithfully if he allowed the Galatian Christians to remain on the wrong track. Whose approval are you seeking—others' or God's? Pray for the courage to seek God's approval above anyone else's.

● **1:11ff** Why should the Galatians have listened to Paul instead of the Judaizers? Paul answered this implicit question by furnishing his credentials: His message was received directly from Christ (1:12); he had been an exemplary Jew (1:13, 14); he had had a special conversion experience (1:15, 16; see also Acts 9:1-9); he had been confirmed and accepted in his ministry by the other apostles (1:18, 19; 2:1-9). Paul also presented his credentials to the Corinthian and Philippian churches (2 Corinthians 11–12; Philippians 3:4-9).

1:12 There are two possible meanings consistent with the grammar of the phrase, "direct revelation from Jesus Christ." (1) This was a revelation by Christ to Paul that spelled out the gospel message, or (2) it was a personal revelation by Christ of his true identity that suddenly confirmed the gospel message against which Paul had been in bitter conflict. Within each meaning the fact remains that God provided the revelation and its content was the gospel.

1:13, 14 Paul had been one of the most religious Jews of his day, scrupulously keeping the law and relentlessly persecuting Christians (see Acts 9:1, 2). Before his conversion Paul had been even more zealous for the law than the Judaizers. He had surpassed his contemporaries in religious knowledge and practice. Paul had been sincere in his zeal—but wrong. When he met Jesus Christ, his life changed. He then directed all his energies toward building up the Christian church.

1:14 To be fully Jewish, a person must have descended from Abraham. In addition, a faithful Jew adhered to the Jewish laws and traditions. Gentiles (1:16) are non-Jews, whether in nationality or religion. In Paul's day, Jews thought of all Gentiles as pagans. Jews avoided Gentiles, believing that contact with Gentiles brought spiritual corruption. Although Gentiles could become Jews in reli-

gion by undergoing circumcision and by following Jewish laws and customs, they were never fully accepted.

Many Jews had difficulty understanding that God's message is for Jews and Gentiles alike. Some Jews thought that Gentiles had to become Jews before they could become Christians. But God planned to save both Jews and Gentiles. He had revealed this plan through Old Testament prophets (see, for example, Genesis 12:3; Isaiah 42:6; 66:19), and he had fulfilled it through Jesus Christ; he was proclaiming it to the Gentiles through Paul.

● **1:15, 16** Because God was guiding his ministry, Paul wasn't doing anything that God hadn't already planned and given him power to do. Similarly, God appointed Jeremiah to be his spokesman even before Jeremiah was born (Jeremiah 1:5). God knows you intimately as well, and he chose you to be his even before you were born (see Psalm 139). He wants you to draw close to him and to fulfill the purpose he has for your life.

● **1:15-24** Paul tells of his conversion to show that his message came directly from God. God commissioned Paul to preach the Good News to the Gentiles. After his call, Paul did not consult with anyone; instead, he spent three years in Arabia. Then he spoke with Peter and James, but he had no other contact with Jewish Christians for several more years. During those years, Paul preached to the Gentiles the message God had given him. His message did not come from human insight; it came from God.

1:18 This was Paul's first visit to Jerusalem as a Christian, as recorded in Acts 9:26-30.

1:21 Because of opposition in Jerusalem (see Acts 9:29, 30), Paul had gone to Syria and Cilicia. In those remote areas, he had no opportunity to receive instruction from the apostles.

1:23 Paul was making the point that his authority and ministry were recognized by people who had never even seen him; yet the Galatians had met him, listened to him, and believed his message, only to turn around and doubt him! The Judean Christians only knew what people were saying: that the one who had persecuted believers was now preaching the faith he had tried to destroy. Instead of doubting Paul's credibility, the churches in Judea had believed and glorified God.

1:24 Paul's changed life had brought praise from those who saw him or heard about him. His new life had astonished them. They

The Apostles Accept Paul

2:1
Acts 15:2

2:2
Gal 1:6

2:3
Acts 16:3

2:4
Gal 1:7; 5:1, 13

2 Then fourteen years later I went back to Jerusalem again, this time with Barnabas; and Titus came along, too. ²I went there because God revealed to me that I should go. While I was there I met privately with those considered to be leaders of the church and shared with them the message I had been preaching to the Gentiles. I wanted to make sure that we were in agreement, for fear that all my efforts had been wasted and I was running the race for nothing. ³And they supported me and did not even demand that my companion Titus be circumcised, though he was a Gentile.*

⁴Even that question came up only because of some so-called Christians there—false ones,

2:3 Greek *a Greek.*

JUDAIZERS VERSUS PAUL

What the Judaizers said about Paul	Paul's defense
They said he was perverting the truth.	He received his message from Christ himself (1:11, 12).
They said he was a traitor to the Jewish faith.	Paul had been one of the most dedicated Jews of his time. Yet, in the midst of one of his most zealous acts, God transformed him through a revelation of the Good News about Jesus (1:13-16; Acts 9:1-30).
They said he compromised and watered down his message for the Gentiles.	The other apostles declared that the message Paul preached was the true gospel (2:1-10).
They said he was disregarding the law of Moses.	Far from degrading the law, Paul puts the law in its proper place. He says it shows people where they have sinned, and it points them to Christ (3:19-29).

As the debate raged between the Gentile Christians and the Judaizers, Paul found it necessary to write to the churches in Galatia. The Judaizers were trying to undermine Paul's authority, and they taught a false gospel. In reply, Paul defended his authority as an apostle and the truth of his message. The debate over Jewish laws and Gentile Christians was officially resolved at the Jerusalem council (Acts 15), yet it continued to be a point of contention after that time.

---

had praised God because only God could have turned this zealous persecutor of Christians into a Christian himself. We may not have had as dramatic a change as Paul, but still our new life should honor God in every way. When people look at you, do they recognize that God has made changes in you? If not, perhaps you are not living as you should.

2:1 Paul was converted around A.D. 35. The 14 years he mentions are probably calculated from the time of his conversion. Therefore, this trip to Jerusalem was not his first. Most likely, he made his first trip to Jerusalem around A.D. 38 (see Acts 9:26-30), and other trips to Jerusalem in approximately A.D. 44 (Acts 11:29, 30; Galatians 2:1-10), A.D. 49/50 (Acts 15), A.D. 52 (Acts 18:22), and A.D. 57 (Acts 21:15ff). Paul probably visited Jerusalem on several other occasions as well.

2:1 Barnabas and Titus were two of Paul's close friends. Barnabas and Paul visited Galatia together on their first missionary journey. Paul wrote a personal letter to Titus, a faithful believer and church leader serving on the island of Crete (see the book of Titus). For more information on Barnabas, see his Profile in Acts 13, p. 1849. For more information on Titus, see the letter Paul wrote to him in the New Testament.

2:1 After his conversion, Paul spent many years preparing for the ministry to which God had called him. This preparation period included time alone with God (1:16, 17), as well as time conferring with other Christians. Often new Christians, in their zeal, want to begin a full-time ministry without investing the necessary time studying the Bible and learning from qualified teachers. We need not wait to share Christ with our friends, but we may need more preparation before embarking on a special ministry, whether volunteer or paid. While we wait for God's timing, we should continue to study, learn, and grow.

• **2:2** God told Paul, through a revelation, to confer with the church leaders in Jerusalem about the message he was preaching to the Gentiles, so they would understand and approve of what he was doing. The essence of Paul's message to both Jews and Gentiles was that God's salvation is offered to all people regardless of race, sex, nationality, wealth, social standing, educational level, or anything else. Anyone can be forgiven by trusting in Christ (see Romans 10:8-13).

• **2:2, 3** Even though God had specifically sent him to the Gentiles (Acts 9:15, 16), Paul needed to discuss his message with the leaders of the Jerusalem church (Acts 15). This meeting prevented a major split in the church, and it formally acknowledged the apostles' approval of Paul's preaching. Sometimes we avoid conferring with others because we fear that problems or arguments may develop. Instead, we should openly discuss our plans and actions with friends, counselors, and advisers. Good communication helps everyone understand the situation better, it reduces gossip, and it builds unity in the church.

2:3-5 When Paul took Titus, a Greek Christian, to Jerusalem, the Judaizers ("false" Christians) said that Titus should be circumcised. Paul adamantly refused to give in to their demands. The apostles agreed that circumcision was an unnecessary rite for Gentile converts. Several years later, Paul circumcised Timothy, another Greek Christian (Acts 16:3). Unlike Titus, however, Timothy was half Jewish. Paul did not deny Jews the right to be circumcised; he was simply saying that Gentiles should not be asked to become Jews before becoming Christians.

2:4 These false Christians were most likely from the party of the Pharisees (Acts 15:5). These were the strictest religious leaders of Judaism, some of whom had been converted. We don't know if these were representatives of well-meaning converts or of those trying to pervert Christianity. Most commentators agree that neither Peter nor James had any part in this conspiracy.

really*—who were secretly brought in. They sneaked in to spy on us and take away the freedom we have in Christ Jesus. They wanted to enslave us and force us to follow their Jewish regulations. ⁵But we refused to give in to them for a single moment. We wanted to preserve the truth of the gospel message for you.

2:5
Gal 1:6; 2:14

⁶And the leaders of the church had nothing to add to what I was preaching. (By the way, their reputation as great leaders made no difference to me, for God has no favorites.) ⁷Instead, they saw that God had given me the responsibility of preaching the gospel to the Gentiles, just as he had given Peter the responsibility of preaching to the Jews. ⁸For the same God who worked through Peter as the apostle to the Jews also worked through me as the apostle to the Gentiles.

2:6
Deut 10:17
Acts 10:34
Rom 2:11
2 Cor 12:11

2:7
Acts 9:15; 22:21
1 Thes 2:4

⁹In fact, James, Peter,* and John, who were known as pillars of the church, recognized the gift God had given me, and they accepted Barnabas and me as their co-workers. They encouraged us to keep preaching to the Gentiles, while they continued their work with the Jews. ¹⁰Their only suggestion was that we keep on helping the poor, which I have always been eager to do.

2:9
Rom 1:5

2:10
Acts 11:29-30;
24:17

Paul Confronts Peter

¹¹But when Peter came to Antioch, I had to oppose him to his face, for what he did was very wrong. ¹²When he first arrived, he ate with the Gentile Christians, who were not circumcised. But afterward, when some friends of James came, Peter wouldn't eat with the Gentiles anymore. He was afraid of criticism from these people who insisted on the necessity of circumcision. ¹³As a result, other Jewish Christians followed Peter's hypocrisy, and even Barnabas was led astray by their hypocrisy.

2:12
Acts 11:2-3

2:14
Acts 10:28

2:15
Phil 3:4-5

¹⁴When I saw that they were not following the truth of the gospel message, I said to Peter in front of all the others, "Since you, a Jew by birth, have discarded the Jewish laws and are living like a Gentile, why are you now trying to make these Gentiles follow the Jewish traditions?

¹⁵"You and I are Jews by birth, not 'sinners' like the Gentiles. ¹⁶Yet we know that a person is

2:16
Acts 15:10-11
Rom 1:17; 3:20, 28;
8:3
Gal 3:11
Eph 2:8

2:4 Greek *some false brothers.*   **2:9** Greek *Cephas;* also in 2:11, 14.

2:5 We normally think of taking a stand against those who might lead us into immoral behavior, but Paul had to take a hard line against the most moral of people. We must not give in to those who make the keeping of man-made standards a condition for salvation, even when such people are morally upright or in respected positions.

• **2:6** It's easy to rate people on the basis of their official status and to be intimidated by powerful people. But Paul was not intimidated by these "great leaders" because all believers are equal in Christ. We should show respect for our spiritual leaders, but our ultimate allegiance must be to Christ. We are to serve him with our whole being. God doesn't rate us according to our status; he looks at the attitude of our hearts (1 Samuel 16:7). We should encourage leaders who show humility and a heartfelt desire to please God.

2:7-9 The church leaders ("pillars")—James (the half-brother of Jesus, not the apostle), Peter, and John—realized that God was using Paul to reach the Gentiles, just as Peter was being used so greatly to reach the Jews. After hearing Paul's message, they gave Paul and Barnabas their approval to continue working among the Gentiles.

2:10 The apostles were referring to the poor of Jerusalem. While many Gentile converts were financially comfortable, the Jerusalem church had suffered from the effects of a severe famine in Palestine (see Acts 11:28-30) and was struggling. So on his journeys, Paul had gathered funds for the Jewish Christians (Acts 24:17; Romans 15:25-29; 1 Corinthians 16:1-4; 2 Corinthians 8). The need for believers to care for the poor is a constant theme in Scripture. But often we do nothing, caught up in meeting our own needs and desires. Perhaps we don't see enough poverty to remember the needs of the poor. The world is filled with poor people, here and in other countries. What can you do to help?

• **2:11** This was Antioch of Syria (distinguished from Antioch in Pisidia), a major trade center in the ancient world. Heavily populated by Greeks, it eventually became a strong Christian center. In Antioch the believers were first called Christians (Acts 11:26).

Antioch of Syria became the headquarters for the Gentile church and was Paul's base of operations.

• **2:11ff** The Judaizers accused Paul of watering down the Good News to make it easier for Gentiles to accept, while Paul accused the Judaizers of nullifying the truth of the Good News by adding conditions to it. The basis of salvation was the issue: Is salvation through Christ alone, or does it come through Christ *and* adherence to the law? The argument came to a climax when Peter, Paul, the Judaizers, and some Gentile Christians all gathered together in Antioch to share a meal. Peter probably thought that by staying away from the Gentiles, he was promoting harmony—he did not want to offend James and the Jewish Christians. James had a very prominent position and presided over the Jerusalem council (Acts 15). But Paul charged that Peter's action violated the Good News. By joining the Judaizers, Peter implicitly was supporting their claim that Christ was not sufficient for salvation. Compromise is an important element in getting along with others, but we should never compromise the truth of God's Word. If we feel we have to change our Christian beliefs to match those of our companions, we are on dangerous ground.

2:11, 12 Although Peter was a leader of the church, he was acting like a hypocrite. He knew better, yet he was driven by fear of what James and the others would think. Proverbs 29:25 says, "Fearing people is a dangerous trap." Paul knew that he had to confront Peter before his actions damaged the church. So, Paul publicly opposed Peter. Note, however, that Paul did not go to the other leaders, nor did he write letters to the churches telling them not to follow Peter's example. Instead, he opposed Peter face to face. Sometimes sincere Christians, even Christian leaders, make mistakes. And it may take other sincere Christians to get them back on track. If you are convinced that someone is doing harm to himself/herself or the church, try the direct approach. There is no place for backstabbing in the body of Christ.

2:15, 16 If observing the Jewish laws cannot justify us, why should we still obey the Ten Commandments and other Old Testa-

made right with God by faith in Jesus Christ, not by obeying the law. And we have believed in Christ Jesus, so that we might be made right with God because of our faith in Christ, not because we have obeyed the law. For no one will ever be made right with God by obeying the law."*

[17]But suppose we seek to be made right with God through faith in Christ and then we are found guilty because we have abandoned the law. Would that mean Christ has led us into sin? Absolutely not! [18]Rather, I am a sinner if I rebuild the old system of law I already tore down. [19]For when I tried to keep the law, it condemned me. So I died to the law—I stopped trying to meet all its requirements—so that I might live for God. [20]My old self has been crucified with Christ.* It is no longer I who live, but Christ lives in me. So I live in this earthly body by trusting in the Son of God, who loved me and gave himself for me. [21]I do not treat the grace of God as meaningless. For if keeping the law could make us right with God, then there was no need for Christ to die.

2. Superiority of the gospel
The Law and Faith in Christ

3 Oh, foolish Galatians! Who has cast an evil spell on you? For the meaning of Jesus Christ's death was made as clear to you as if you had seen a picture of his death on the cross. [2]Let me ask you this one question: Did you receive the Holy Spirit by obeying the law of Moses? Of course not! You received the Spirit because you believed the message you heard about Christ. [3]How foolish can you be? After starting your Christian lives in the Spirit, why are you now trying to become perfect by your own human effort? [4]Have you experienced* so much for nothing? Surely it was not in vain, was it?

[5]I ask you again, does God give you the Holy Spirit and work miracles among you because you obey the law? Of course not! It is because you believe the message you heard about Christ.

2:16 Some translators hold that the quotation extends through verse 14; others through verse 16; and still others through verse 21.   **2:20** Some English translations put this sentence in verse 19.   **3:4** Or *Have you suffered.*

2:19
Rom 6:10-14; 7:4
2 Cor 5:15
2:20
Rom 6:6; 8:37
Gal 1:4
1 Tim 2:6
Titus 2:14

3:1
1 Cor 1:23
Gal 5:7
3:2
Rom 10:17
3:3
Gal 4:9
3:4
2 Jn 1:8
3:5
1 Cor 12:10

---

ment laws? We know that Paul was not saying the law is bad, because in another letter he wrote, "The law itself is holy, and its commands are holy and right and good" (Romans 7:12). Instead, he is saying that the law can never make us acceptable to God. The law still has an important role to play in the life of a Christian. The law (1) guards us from sin by giving us standards for behavior; (2) convicts us of sin, leaving us the opportunity to ask for God's forgiveness; and (3) drives us to trust in the sufficiency of Christ, because we can never keep the Ten Commandments perfectly. The law cannot possibly save us. But after we become Christians, it can guide us to live as God requires.

2:17-19 Through studying the Old Testament Scriptures, Paul realized that he could not be saved by obeying God's laws. The prophets knew that God's plan of salvation did not rest on keeping the law (see the chart in chapter 3, p. 1989 for references). Because we have all been infected by sin, we cannot keep God's laws perfectly. Fortunately, God has provided a way of salvation that depends on Jesus Christ, not on our own efforts. Even though we know this truth, we must guard against the temptation of using service, good deeds, charitable giving, or any other effort as a substitute for faith.

2:19, 20 How have our old selves been crucified with Christ? *Legally*, God looks at us as if we had died with Christ. Because our sins died with him, we are no longer condemned (Colossians 2:13-15). *Relationally*, we have become one with Christ, and his experiences are ours. Our Christian life began when, in unity with him, we died to our old life (see Romans 6:5-11). *In our daily life*, we must regularly crucify sinful desires that keep us from following Christ. This, too, is a kind of dying with him (Luke 9:23-25).

And yet the focus of Christianity is not on dying but on living. Because we have been crucified with Christ, we have also been raised with him (Romans 6:5). *Legally*, we have been reconciled with God (2 Corinthians 5:19) and are free to grow into Christ's likeness (Romans 8:29). And *in our daily life*, we have Christ's resurrection power as we continue to fight sin (Ephesians 1:19, 20). We are no longer alone, for Christ lives in us—he is our power for living and our hope for the future (Colossians 1:27).

2:21 Believers today may still be in danger of acting as if there was no need for Christ to die. How? By replacing Jewish legalism with their own brand of Christian legalism, they are giving people extra laws to obey. By believing they can earn God's favor by what they do, they are not trusting completely in Christ's work on the cross. By struggling to appropriate God's power to change them (sanctification), they are not resting in God's power to save them (justification). If we could be saved by being good, then Christ would not have had to die. But the cross is the only way to salvation.

3:1 The Galatian believers had become fascinated by the false teachers' arguments, almost as though an evil spell had been cast on them. Magic was common in Paul's day (Acts 8:9-11; 13:6, 7). Magicians used both optical illusions and Satan's power to perform miracles, and people were drawn into the magicians' mysterious rites without recognizing their dangerous source.

• **3:2, 3** Some of the believers in Galatia may have been in Jerusalem at Pentecost and received the Holy Spirit there. They knew that they hadn't received God's Spirit by obeying the Jewish laws. Paul stressed that just as they began their Christian lives in the power of the Spirit, so they should grow by the Spirit's power. The Galatians had taken a step backward when they had decided to insist on keeping the Jewish laws. We must realize that we grow spiritually because of God's work in us by his Spirit, not by following special rules.

• **3:5** The Galatians knew that they had received the Holy Spirit when they believed, not when they obeyed the law. People still feel insecure in their faith because faith alone seems too easy. People still try to get closer to God by following rules. While certain disciplines (Bible study, prayer) and service may help us grow, they must not take the place of the Holy Spirit in us or become ends in themselves. By asking these questions, Paul hoped to get the Galatians to focus again on Christ as the foundation of their faith.

• **3:5** The Holy Spirit gives Christians great power to live for God. Some Christians want more than this. They want to live in a state of perpetual excitement. The tedium of everyday living leads them to conclude that something is wrong spiritually. Often the Holy Spirit's greatest work is teaching us to persist, to keep on doing what is right even when it no longer seems interesting or exciting. The Galatians quickly turned from Paul's Good News to the teachings of the newest teachers in town; what they needed was the Holy Spirit's gift of persistence. If the Christian life seems ordinary, you may need the Spirit to stir you up. Every day offers a challenge to live for Christ.

⁶In the same way, "Abraham believed God, and God counted him as righteous because of his faith."* ⁷The real children of Abraham, then, are those who put their faith in God.

⁸What's more, the Scriptures looked forward to this time when God would declare the Gentiles to be righteous because of their faith. God proclaimed this good news to Abraham long ago when he said, "All nations will be blessed through you."* ⁹So all who put their faith in Christ share the same blessing Abraham received because of his faith.

¹⁰But those who depend on the law to make them right with God are under his curse, for the Scriptures say, "Cursed is everyone who does not observe and obey all the commands that are written in God's Book of the Law."* ¹¹So it is clear that no one can be made right with God by trying to keep the law. For the Scriptures say, "It is through faith that a righteous person has life."* ¹²This way of faith is very different from the way of law, which says, "It is through obeying the law that a person has life."*

¹³But Christ has rescued us from the curse pronounced by the law. When he was hung on the cross, he took upon himself the curse for our wrongdoing. For it is written in the Scriptures, "Cursed is everyone who is hung on a tree."* ¹⁴Through Christ Jesus, God has blessed the Gentiles with the same blessing he promised to Abraham, so that we who are believers might receive the promised* Holy Spirit through faith.

The Law and God's Promise

¹⁵Dear brothers and sisters,* here's an example from everyday life. Just as no one can set aside or amend an irrevocable agreement, so it is in this case. ¹⁶God gave the promises to Abraham and his child.* And notice that the Scripture doesn't say "to his children,*" as if it meant many descendants. Rather, it says "to his child"—and that, of course, means Christ. ¹⁷This is what I am trying to say: The agreement God made with Abraham could not be canceled 430 years later when God gave the law to Moses. God would be breaking his promise. ¹⁸For if the inheritance could be received by keeping the law, then it would not be the result of accepting God's promise. But God graciously gave it to Abraham as a promise.

¹⁹Why, then, was the law given? It was given alongside the promise to show people their sins. But the law was designed to last only until the coming of the child who was promised. God gave his law through angels to Moses, who was the mediator between God and the people. ²⁰Now a mediator is helpful if more than one party must reach an agreement. But God, who is one, did not use a mediator when he gave his promise to Abraham.

Marginal cross-references:
3:6 †Gen 15:6 / Rom 4:3
3:8 †Gen 12:3 / Acts 3:25
3:10 †Deut 27:26 / Jer 11:3
3:11 †Hab 2:4 / Rom 1:17 / Heb 10:38
3:12 †Lev 18:5 / Rom 10:5
3:13 †Deut 21:23 / Gal 4:5
3:14 Joel 2:28 / Acts 2:33
3:15 Heb 9:17
3:16 †Gen 12:7; 13:15; 17:7; 24:7
3:17 Exod 12:40
3:18 Rom 4:14; 11:6
3:19 Exod 20:19 / Deut 5:5 / Acts 7:53 / Heb 2:2
3:20 1 Tim 2:5

3:6 Gen 15:6. **3:8** Gen 12:3; 18:18; 22:18. **3:10** Deut 27:26. **3:11** Hab 2:4. **3:12** Lev 18:5. **3:13** Deut 21:23 (Greek version). **3:14** Some manuscripts read *the blessing of the.* **3:15** Greek *Brothers.* **3:16a** Greek *seed;* also in 3:16c, 19. See notes on Gen 12:7 and 13:15. **3:16b** Greek *seeds.*

3:6-9 The main argument of the Judaizers was that Gentiles had to become Jews in order to become Christians. Paul exposed the flaw in this argument by showing that real children of Abraham are those who have faith, not those who keep the law. Abraham himself was saved by his faith (Genesis 15:6). All believers in every age and from every nation share Abraham's blessing. This is a comforting promise, a great heritage for us, and a solid foundation for living.

• **3:10** Paul quoted Deuteronomy 27:26 to prove that, contrary to what the Judaizers claimed, the law cannot justify and save— it can only condemn. Breaking even one commandment brings a person under condemnation. And because everyone has broken the commandments, everyone stands condemned. The law can do nothing to reverse the condemnation (Romans 3:20-24). But Christ took the curse of the law upon himself when he hung on the cross. He did this so we wouldn't have to bear our own punishment. The only condition is that we accept Christ's death on our behalf as the means to be saved (Colossians 1:20-23).

• **3:11** Trying to be right with God by our own effort doesn't work. Good intentions such as "I'll do better next time" or "I'll never do that again" usually end in failure. Paul points to Habakkuk's declaration (Habakkuk 2:4) that by trusting God—believing in his provision for our sins and living each day in his power—we can break this cycle of failure.

3:17 In the same way that we claim Jesus' death as God's provision for our salvation, Abraham believed in God and his promises, although they would not be made fully evident until centuries later on the cross. God promised, and Abraham answered in faith, even during the trial of God asking him to sacrifice his son. This is the heart of Christian faith. God promises to save us when we trust in Christ and take him at his word, just as Abraham did. We *know* in greater detail how God worked out his plan of grace in Christ. We have much less excuse for our unbelief!

• **3:18, 19** The law has two functions. On the positive side, it reveals the nature and will of God and shows people how to live. On the negative side, it points out people's sins and shows them that it is impossible to please God by trying to obey all his laws completely. God's promise to Abraham dealt with Abraham's faith; the law focuses on actions. The covenant with Abraham shows that faith is the only way to be saved; the law shows how to obey God in grateful response. Faith does not annul the law; but the more we know God, the more we see how sinful we are. Then we are driven to depend on our faith in Christ alone for our salvation.

• **3:19, 20** When God gave his promise to Abraham, he did it by himself alone, without angels or Moses as mediators. Although it is not mentioned in Exodus, Jews believed that the Ten Commandments had been given to Moses by angels (Stephen referred to this in his speech, see Acts 7:38, 53). Paul was showing the superiority of salvation and growth by faith over trying to be saved by keeping the Jewish laws. Christ is the best and only way given by God for us to come to him (1 Timothy 2:5).

3:21
Rom 8:2-4
3:22
Rom 3:11-19;
11:32

²¹Is there a conflict, then, between God's law and God's promises?* Absolutely not! If the law could give us new life, we could be made right with God by obeying it. ²²But the Scriptures declare that we are all prisoners of sin, so we receive God's promise of freedom only by believing in Jesus Christ.

God's Children through Faith

²³Before the way of faith in Christ was available to us, we were placed under guard by the law. We were kept in protective custody, so to speak, until the way of faith was revealed.

3:24
Rom 10:4
3:27
Rom 6:3; 13:14
3:28
John 10:16; 17:21
1 Cor 12:13
Eph 2:14-15
Col 3:11
3:29
Rom 8:17
Gal 3:16

²⁴Let me put it another way. The law was our guardian until Christ came; it protected us until we could be made right with God through faith. ²⁵And now that the way of faith has come, we no longer need the law as our guardian.

²⁶For you are all children* of God through faith in Christ Jesus. ²⁷And all who have been united with Christ in baptism have put on Christ, like putting on new clothes.* ²⁸There is no longer Jew or Gentile,* slave or free, male and female. For you are all one in Christ Jesus. ²⁹And now that you belong to Christ, you are the true children* of Abraham. You are his heirs, and God's promise to Abraham belongs to you.

3:21 Some manuscripts read *and the promises?* **3:26** Greek *sons.* **3:27** Greek *have put on Christ.* **3:28** Greek *Jew or Greek.* **3:29** Greek *seed.*

DO WE STILL HAVE TO OBEY THE OLD TESTAMENT LAWS?

When Paul says that non-Jews (Gentiles) are no longer bound by these laws, he is not saying that the Old Testament laws do not apply to us today. He is saying certain types of laws may not apply to us. In the Old Testament there were three categories of laws:

Ceremonial law	This kind of law relates specifically to Israel's worship (see, for example, Leviticus 1:1-13). Its primary purpose was to point forward to Jesus Christ. Therefore, these laws were no longer necessary after Jesus' death and resurrection. While we are no longer bound by ceremonial laws, the principles behind them—to worship and love a holy God—still apply. The Jewish Christians often accused the Gentile Christians of violating the ceremonial law.
Civil law	This type of law dictated Israel's daily living (see Deuteronomy 24:10, 11, for example). Because modern society and culture are so radically different, some of these guidelines cannot be followed specifically. But the principles behind the commands should guide our conduct. At times, Paul asked Gentile Christians to follow some of these laws, not because they had to, but in order to promote unity.
Moral law	This sort of law is the direct command of God—for example, the Ten Commandments (Exodus 20:1-17). It requires strict obedience. It reveals the nature and will of God, and it still applies to us today. We are to obey this moral law, not to obtain salvation, but to live in ways pleasing to God.

● **3:21, 22** Before faith in Christ delivered us, we were imprisoned by sin, beaten down by past mistakes, and choked by desires that we knew were wrong. God knew we were sin's prisoners, but he provided a way of escape—faith in Jesus Christ. Without Christ, everyone is held in sin's grasp, and only those who place their faith in Christ ever get out of it. Look to Christ—he is reaching out to set you free.

● **3:24, 25** The picture of the law as a guardian is similar to a tutor giving a young child supervision. We no longer need that kind of supervision. The law teaches us the *need* for salvation; God's grace *gives* us that salvation. The Old Testament still applies today. In it, God reveals his nature, his will for humanity, his moral laws, and his guidelines for living. But we cannot be saved by keeping that law; we must trust in Christ.

● **3:28** Some Jewish males greeted each new day by praying, "Lord, I thank you that I am not a Gentile, a slave, or a woman." The role of women was enhanced by Christianity. Faith in Christ transcends these differences and makes all believers one in Christ. Make sure you do not impose distinctions that Christ has removed. Because all believers are his heirs, no one is more privileged than or superior to anyone else.

● **3:28** It's our natural inclination to feel uncomfortable around people who are different from us and to gravitate toward those who are similar to us. But when we allow our differences to separate us from our fellow believers, we are disregarding clear biblical teaching. Make a point to seek out and appreciate people who are not just like you and your friends. You may find that you have a lot in common with them.

3:29 The original promise to Abraham was intended for the whole world, not just for Abraham's physical descendants (see Genesis 12:3). All believers participate in this promise and are blessed as children of Abraham.

4 Think of it this way. If a father dies and leaves an inheritance for his young children, those children are not much better off than slaves until they grow up, even though they actually own everything their father had. ²They have to obey their guardians until they reach whatever age their father set. ³And that's the way it was with us before Christ came. We were like children; we were slaves to the basic spiritual principles* of this world.

⁴But when the right time came, God sent his Son, born of a woman, subject to the law. ⁵God sent him to buy freedom for us who were slaves to the law, so that he could adopt us as his very own children.* ⁶And because we* are his children, God has sent the Spirit of his Son into our hearts, prompting us to call out, "Abba, Father."* ⁷Now you are no longer a slave but God's own child.* And since you are his child, God has made you his heir.

Paul's Concern for the Galatians

⁸Before you Gentiles knew God, you were slaves to so-called gods that do not even exist. ⁹So now that you know God (or should I say, now that God knows you), why do you want to go back again and become slaves once more to the weak and useless spiritual principles of this world? ¹⁰You are trying to earn favor with God by observing certain days or months or seasons or years. ¹¹I fear for you. Perhaps all my hard work with you was for nothing. ¹²Dear brothers and sisters,* I plead with you to live as I do in freedom from these things, for I have become like you Gentiles—free from those laws.

You did not mistreat me when I first preached to you. ¹³Surely you remember that I was sick when I first brought you the Good News. ¹⁴But even though my condition tempted you to reject me, you did not despise me or turn me away. No, you took me in and cared for me as though I were an angel from God or even Christ Jesus himself. ¹⁵Where is that joyful and grateful spirit you felt then? I am sure you would have taken out your own eyes and given them to me if it had been possible. ¹⁶Have I now become your enemy because I am telling you the truth?

4:3 Gal 3:23
Col 2:8, 20
4:4 Mark 1:15
John 1:14
Eph 1:10
Heb 2:14
4:5 Rom 8:15
Eph 1:5
4:6 Rom 8:15-16
4:7 Rom 8:17
4:8 2 Chr 13:9
Isa 37:19
Jer 2:11
1 Cor 8:4-6
1 Thes 1:9
4:9 Col 2:20
4:10 Rom 14:5
Col 2:16
4:13 1 Cor 2:3
4:14 Matt 10:40
4:16 Amos 5:10

4:3 Or *powers;* also in 4:9. **4:5** Greek *sons;* also in 4:6. **4:6a** Greek *you.* **4:6b** *Abba* is an Aramaic term for "father." **4:7** Greek *son;* also in 4:7b. **4:12** Greek *brothers;* also in 4:28, 31.

• **4:3-7** Paul uses the illustration of slavery to show that before Christ came and died for sins, people were in bondage to the law. Thinking they could be saved by it, they became enslaved to trying—and failing—to keep it. But we who were once slaves are now God's very own children who have an intimate relationship with him. Because of Christ, there is no reason to be afraid of God. We can come boldly into his presence, knowing that he will welcome us as his family members.

4:4 "When the right time came," God sent Jesus to earth to die for our sins. For centuries the Jews had been wondering when their Messiah would come—but God's timing was perfect. We may sometimes wonder if God will ever respond to our prayers. But we must never doubt him or give up hope. At the right time he will respond. Are you waiting for God's timing? Trust his judgment and trust that he has your best interests in mind.

4:4, 5 Jesus was born of a woman—he was human. He was born as a Jew—he was subject to God's law and fulfilled it perfectly. Thus, Jesus was the perfect sacrifice because, although he was fully human, he never sinned. His death bought freedom for us who were enslaved to sin so that we could be adopted into God's family.

• **4:5-7** Under Roman law, an adopted child was guaranteed all legal rights to his father's property, even if he was formerly a slave. He was not a second-class son; he was equal to all other sons, biological or adopted, in his father's family. As adopted children of God, we share with Jesus all rights to God's resources. As God's heirs, we can claim what he has provided for us—our full identity as his children (see Romans 8:15-17).

4:13, 14 Paul's illness was a sickness that he was enduring while he visited the Galatian churches. The world is often callous to people's pain and misery. Paul commended the Galatians for not scorning him, even though his condition was a trial to them (he didn't explain what was wrong with him). Such caring was what Jesus meant when he called us to serve the homeless, hungry, sick, and imprisoned as if they were Jesus himself (Matthew 25:34-40). Do you avoid those in pain or those facing difficulty—or are you willing to care for them as if they were Jesus Christ himself?

• **4:15** Have you lost your joy? Paul sensed that the Galatians had lost the joy of their salvation because of legalism. Legalism can take away joy because (1) it makes people feel guilty rather than loved; (2) it produces self-hatred rather than humility; (3) it stresses performance over relationship; (4) it points out how far short we fall rather than how far we've come because of what Christ did for us. If you feel guilty and inadequate, check your focus. Are you living by faith in Christ or by trying to live up to the demands and expectations of others?

4:16 Paul did not gain great popularity when he rebuked the Galatians for turning away from their first faith in Christ. Human nature hasn't changed much—we still get angry when we're scolded. But don't write off someone who challenges you. There may be truth in what he or she says. Receive his or her words with humility; carefully think them over. If you discover that you need to change an attitude or action, take steps to do it.

4:17
Gal 2:4, 12

¹⁷Those false teachers are so eager to win your favor, but their intentions are not good. They are trying to shut you off from me so that you will pay attention only to them. ¹⁸If someone is eager to do good things for you, that's all right; but let them do it all the time, not just when I'm with you.

4:19
Eph 4:13

¹⁹Oh, my dear children! I feel as if I'm going through labor pains for you again, and they will continue until Christ is fully developed in your lives. ²⁰I wish I were with you right now so I could change my tone. But at this distance I don't know how else to help you.

THREE DISTORTIONS OF CHRISTIANITY	Group	Their definition of a Christian	Their genuine concern	The danger	Application question
Almost from the beginning there were forces at work within Christianity that would have destroyed or sidetracked the movement. Of these, three created many problems then and have continued to reappear in other forms even today. The three aberrations are contrasted to true Christianity.	Judaized Christianity	Christians are Jews who have recognized Jesus as the promised Savior. Therefore, any Gentile desiring to become a Christian must first become a Jew.	Having a high regard for the Scriptures and God's choice of Jews as his people, they did not want to see God's commands overlooked or broken.	Tends to add human traditions and standards to God's law. Also subtracts from the Scriptures God's clear concern for all nations.	Do you appreciate God's choice of a unique people through whom he offered forgiveness and eternal life to all peoples?
	Legalized Christianity	Christians are those who live by a long list of "don'ts." God's favor is earned by good behavior.	Recognized that real change brought about by God should lead to changes in behavior.	Tends to make God's love something to earn rather than to accept freely. Would reduce Christianity to a set of impossible rules and transform the Good News into bad news.	As important as change in action is, can you see that God may be desiring different changes in you than in others?
	Lawless Christianity	Christians live above the law. They need no guidelines. God's Word is not as important as our personal sense of God's guidance.	Recognized that forgiveness from God cannot be based on our ability to live up to his perfect standards. It must be received by faith as a gift made possible by Christ's death on the cross.	Forgets that Christians are still human and fail consistently when trying to live only by what they "feel" God wants.	Do you recognize the ongoing need for God's expressed commands as you live out your gratitude for his great salvation?
	True Christianity	Christians are those who believe inwardly and outwardly that Jesus' death has allowed God to offer them forgiveness and eternal life as a gift. They have accepted that gift through faith and are seeking to live a life of obedient gratitude for what God has done for them.	Christianity is both private and public, with heart-belief and mouth-confession. Our relationship to God and the power he provides result in obedience. Having received forgiveness and eternal life, we are now daily challenged to live that life with his help.	Avoids the above dangers.	How would those closest to you describe your Christianity? Do they think you live *so* that God will accept you, or do they know that you live *because* God has accepted you in Christ?

• **4:17** The false teachers claimed to be religious authorities and experts in Judaism and Christianity. Appealing to the believers' desire to do what was right, they drew quite a following. Paul said, however, that they were wrong and that their motives were selfish. False teachers are often respectable and persuasive. That is why all teachings should be checked against the Bible.

• **4:19** Paul led many people to Christ and helped them mature spiritually. Perhaps one reason for his success as a spiritual father was the deep concern he felt for his spiritual children; he compared his pain over their faithlessness to the pain of childbirth. We should have the same intense care for those to whom we are spiritual parents. When you lead people to Christ, remember to stand by them to help them grow.

Abraham's Two Children

21 Tell me, you who want to live under the law, do you know what the law actually says? 22 The Scriptures say that Abraham had two sons, one from his slave wife and one from his freeborn wife.* 23 The son of the slave wife was born in a human attempt to bring about the fulfillment of God's promise. But the son of the freeborn wife was born as God's own fulfillment of his promise.

24 These two women serve as an illustration of God's two covenants. The first woman, Hagar, represents Mount Sinai where people received the law that enslaved them. 25 And now Jerusalem is just like Mount Sinai in Arabia,* because she and her children live in slavery to the law. 26 But the other woman, Sarah, represents the heavenly Jerusalem. She is the free woman, and she is our mother. 27 As Isaiah said,

> "Rejoice, O childless woman,
>   you who have never given birth!
> Break into a joyful shout,
>   you who have never been in labor!
> For the desolate woman now has more children
>   than the woman who lives with her husband!"*

28 And you, dear brothers and sisters, are children of the promise, just like Isaac. 29 But you are now being persecuted by those who want you to keep the law, just as Ishmael, the child born by human effort, persecuted Isaac, the child born by the power of the Spirit. 30 But what do the Scriptures say about that? "Get rid of the slave and her son, for the son of the slave woman will not share the inheritance with the free woman's son."* 31 So, dear brothers and sisters, we are not children of the slave woman; we are children of the free woman.

3. Freedom of the gospel

Freedom in Christ

5 So Christ has truly set us free. Now make sure that you stay free, and don't get tied up again in slavery to the law.

2 Listen! I, Paul, tell you this: If you are counting on circumcision to make you right with God, then Christ will be of no benefit to you. 3 I'll say it again. If you are trying to find favor with God by being circumcised, you must obey every regulation in the whole law of Moses. 4 For if you are trying to make yourselves right with God by keeping the law, you have been cut off from Christ! You have fallen away from God's grace.

5 But we who live by the Spirit eagerly wait to receive by faith the righteousness God has promised to us. 6 For when we place our faith in Christ Jesus, there is no benefit in being circumcised or being uncircumcised. What is important is faith expressing itself in love.

4:22 Gen 16:15; 21:2
4:23 Rom 9:7-9
4:26 Heb 12:22; Rev 3:12; 21:2, 10
4:27 †Isa 54:1
4:28 Gal 3:29
4:29 Gen 21:9
4:30 Gen 21:10; John 8:35
4:31 Gal 3:29
5:1 John 8:32, 36; Acts 15:10; Gal 2:4
5:2 Acts 15:1
5:3 Gal 3:10
5:5 Rom 8:23-24
5:6 1 Cor 7:19; 1 Thes 1:3

4:22 See Gen 16:15; 21:2-3.   **4:25** Greek *And Hagar, which is Mount Sinai in Arabia, is now like Jerusalem;* other manuscripts read *And Mount Sinai in Arabia is now like Jerusalem.*   **4:27** Isa 54:1.   **4:30** Gen 21:10.

4:21ff People are saved because of their faith in Christ, not because of what they do. Paul contrasted those who are enslaved to the law (represented by Hagar, the slave wife) with those who are free from the law (represented by Sarah, the freeborn wife). Hagar's abuse of Sarah (Genesis 16:4) was like the persecution that the Gentile Christians were getting from the Judaizers, who insisted on keeping the law in order to be saved. Eventually Sarah triumphed because God kept his promise to give her a son, just as those who worship Christ in faith will also triumph.

4:24 Paul explained that what happened to Sarah and Hagar is an allegory or picture of the relationship between God and people. Paul was using a type of argument that was common in his day and that was probably being used against him by his opponents.

5:1 Christ died to set us free from sin and from a long list of laws and regulations. Christ came to set us free—not free to do whatever we want because that would lead us back into slavery to our selfish desires. Rather, thanks to Christ, we are now free and able to do what was impossible before—to live unselfishly. Those who appeal to their freedom so that they can have their own way or indulge their own desires are falling back into sin. But it is also wrong to put a burden of law-keeping on Christians. We must stand against those who would enslave us with rules, methods, or special conditions for being saved or growing in Christ.

5:2-4 Trying to be saved by keeping the law and being saved by grace are two entirely different approaches. "Christ will be of no benefit to you" means that Christ's provision for our salvation will not help us if we are trying to save ourselves. Obeying the law does not make it any easier for God to save us. All we can do is accept his gracious gift through faith. Our deeds of service must never be used to try to earn God's love or favor.

5:3, 4 Circumcision was a symbol of having the right background and doing everything required by religion. No amount of work, discipline, or moral behavior can save us. If a person were counting on finding favor with God by being circumcised, he would also have to obey the rest of God's law completely. Trying to save ourselves by keeping all God's laws only separates us from God.

• **5:6** We are saved by faith, not by deeds. But love for others and for God is the response of those whom God has forgiven. God's forgiveness is complete, and Jesus said that those who are forgiven much love much (Luke 7:47). Because faith expresses itself through love, you can check your love for others as a way to monitor your faith.

5:7
1 Cor 9:24

5:8
Rom 8:28

5:9
1 Cor 5:6

5:10
Gal 1:7

5:11
1 Cor 1:23

5:13
1 Pet 2:16

5:14
†Lev 19:18
Rom 13:9

⁷You were running the race so well. Who has held you back from following the truth? ⁸It certainly isn't God, for he is the one who called you to freedom. ⁹This false teaching is like a little yeast that spreads through the whole batch of dough! ¹⁰I am trusting the Lord to keep you from believing false teachings. God will judge that person, whoever he is, who has been confusing you.

¹¹Dear brothers and sisters,* if I were still preaching that you must be circumcised—as some say I do—why am I still being persecuted? If I were no longer preaching salvation through the cross of Christ, no one would be offended. ¹²I just wish that those troublemakers who want to mutilate you by circumcision would mutilate themselves.*

¹³For you have been called to live in freedom, my brothers and sisters. But don't use your freedom to satisfy your sinful nature. Instead, use your freedom to serve one another in love. ¹⁴For the whole law can be summed up in this one command: "Love your neighbor as yourself."* ¹⁵But if you are always biting and devouring one another, watch out! Beware of destroying one another.

5:11 Greek *Brothers;* similarly in 5:13.   **5:12** Or *castrate themselves,* or *cut themselves off from you;* Greek reads *cut themselves off.*   **5:14** Lev 19:18.

VICES AND VIRTUES
The Bible mentions many specific actions and attitudes that are either right or wrong. Look at the list included here. Are there a number of characteristics from the wrong column that are influencing you?

VICES
(Neglecting God and others)

Sexual immorality *(Galatians 5:19)*
Impurity *(Galatians 5:19)*
Lust *(Colossians 3:5)*
Hostility *(Galatians 5:20)*
Quarreling *(Galatians 5:20)*
Jealousy *(Galatians 5:20)*
Anger *(Galatians 5:20)*
Selfish ambition *(Galatians 5:20)*
Dissension *(Galatians 5:20)*
Arrogance *(2 Corinthians 12:20)*
Envy *(Galatians 5:21)*
Murder *(Revelation 22:12-16)*
Idolatry *(Galatians 5:20; Ephesians 5:5)*
Sorcery *(Galatians 5:20)*
Drunkenness *(Galatians 5:21)*
Wild parties *(Luke 15:13; Galatians 5:21)*
Cheating *(1 Corinthians 6:8)*
Adultery *(1 Corinthians 6:9, 10)*
Homosexuality *(1 Corinthians 6:9, 10)*
Greed *(1 Corinthians 6:9, 10; Ephesians 5:5)*
Stealing *(1 Corinthians 6:9, 10)*
Lying *(Revelation 22:12-16)*

VIRTUES
(The by-products of living for God)

Love *(Galatians 5:22)*
Joy *(Galatians 5:22)*
Peace *(Galatians 5:22)*
Patience *(Galatians 5:22)*
Kindness *(Galatians 5:22)*
Goodness *(Galatians 5:22)*
Faithfulness *(Galatians 5:22)*
Gentleness *(Galatians 5:23)*
Self-control *(Galatians 5:23)*

5:9 A little yeast causes a whole lump of dough to rise. It only takes one wrong person to infect all the others.

5:11 Persecution proved that Paul was preaching the true Good News. If he had taught what the false teachers were teaching, no one would be offended. But because he was teaching the truth, he was persecuted by both Jews and Judaizers. Have friends or loved ones rejected you because you have taken a stand for Christ? Jesus said not to be surprised if the world hates you, because it hated him (John 15:18, 19). Just as Paul continued to faithfully proclaim the message about Christ, you should continue doing the ministry God has given you—in spite of the obstacles others may put in your way.

• **5:13** Paul distinguishes between freedom to sin and freedom to serve. Freedom or license to sin is no freedom at all, because it enslaves you to Satan, others, or your own sinful nature. Christians, by contrast, should not be slaves to sin, because they are free to do right and to glorify God through loving service to others.

5:14, 15 When we believers lose the motivation of love, we become critical of others. We stop looking for good in them

and see only their faults. Soon we lose our unity. Have you talked behind someone's back? Have you focused on others' shortcomings instead of their strengths? Remind yourself of Jesus' command to love others as you love yourself (Matthew 22:39). When you begin to feel critical of someone, make a list of that person's positive qualities. When problems need to be addressed, confront in love rather than gossip.

Living by the Spirit's Power

16So I say, let the Holy Spirit guide your lives. Then you won't be doing what your sinful nature craves. 17The sinful nature wants to do evil, which is just the opposite of what the Spirit wants. And the Spirit gives us desires that are the opposite of what the sinful nature desires. These two forces are constantly fighting each other, so you are not free to carry out your good intentions. 18But when you are directed by the Spirit, you are not under obligation to the law of Moses.

19When you follow the desires of your sinful nature, the results are very clear: sexual immorality, impurity, lustful pleasures, 20idolatry, sorcery, hostility, quarreling, jealousy, outbursts of anger, selfish ambition, dissension, division, 21envy, drunkenness, wild parties, and other sins like these. Let me tell you again, as I have before, that anyone living that sort of life will not inherit the Kingdom of God.

22But the Holy Spirit produces this kind of fruit in our lives: love, joy, peace, patience, kindness, goodness, faithfulness, 23gentleness, and self-control. There is no law against these things!

24Those who belong to Christ Jesus have nailed the passions and desires of their sinful nature to his cross and crucified them there. 25Since we are living by the Spirit, let us follow the Spirit's leading in every part of our lives. 26Let us not become conceited, or provoke one another, or be jealous of one another.

5:16
Rom 8:4-6
5:17
Rom 7:15-23
5:18
Rom 6:14; 8:14
5:19-21
Rom 13:12-13
1 Cor 6:9-10
Eph 5:5
Rev 22:15
5:22
Eph 5:9
5:24
Rom 6:6
Col 3:5
5:25
Rom 8:4
Gal 5:16
5:26
Phil 2:3

We Harvest What We Plant

6 Dear brothers and sisters, if another believer* is overcome by some sin, you who are godly* should gently and humbly help that person back onto the right path. And be careful not to fall into the same temptation yourself. 2Share each other's burdens, and in this way obey the law of Christ. 3If you think you are too important to help someone, you are only fooling yourself. You are not that important.

6:1
1 Cor 2:15
Jas 5:19-20
1 Jn 5:16
6:2
Rom 15:1
6:3
Rom 12:3
1 Cor 3:18

6:1a Greek *Brothers, if a man.*   **6:1b** Greek *spiritual.*

• **5:16-18** If your desire is to have the qualities listed in 5:22, 23, then you know that the Holy Spirit is leading you. At the same time, be careful not to confuse your subjective feelings with the Spirit's leading. Being led by the Holy Spirit involves the desire to hear, the readiness to obey God's Word, and the sensitivity to discern between your feelings and his promptings. Live each day controlled and guided by the Holy Spirit. Then the words of Christ will be in your mind, the love of Christ will be behind your actions, and the power of Christ will help you control your selfish desires.

• **5:17** Paul describes the two forces fighting within us—the Holy Spirit and the sinful nature (our evil desires or inclinations that stem from our body; see also 5:16, 19, 24). Paul is not saying that these forces are equal—the Holy Spirit is infinitely stronger. But if we rely on our own wisdom, we will make wrong choices. If we try to follow the Spirit by our own human effort, we will fail. Our only way to freedom from our evil desires is through the empowering of the Holy Spirit (see Romans 8:9; Ephesians 4:23, 24; Colossians 3:3-8).

• **5:19-21** We all have evil desires, and we can't ignore them. In order for us to follow the Holy Spirit's guidance, we must deal with them decisively (crucify them—5:24). These desires include obvious sins, such as sexual immorality and demonic activities. They also include less obvious sins, such as hostility, jealousy, and selfish ambition. Those who ignore such sins or refuse to deal with them reveal that they have not received the gift of the Spirit that leads to a transformed life.

• **5:22, 23** The fruit of the Spirit is the spontaneous work of the Holy Spirit in us. The Spirit produces these character traits that are found in the nature of Christ. They are the by-products of Christ's control—we can't obtain them by *trying* to get them without his help. If we want the fruit of the Spirit to grow in us, we must join our life to his (see John 15:4, 5). We must know him, love him, remember him, and imitate him. As a result, we will fulfill the intended purpose of the law—to love God and our neighbors. Which of these qualities do you want the Spirit to produce in you?

• **5:23** Because the God who sent the law also sent the Spirit, the by-products of the Spirit-filled life are in perfect harmony with the intent of God's law. A person who exhibits the fruit of the Spirit fulfills the law far better than a person who observes the rituals but has little love in his or her heart.

• **5:24** In order to accept Christ as Savior, we need to turn from our sins and willingly nail our sinful nature to the cross. This doesn't mean, however, that we will never see traces of its evil desires again. As Christians we still have the capacity to sin, but we have been set free from sin's power over us and no longer have to give in to it. We must daily commit our sinful tendencies to God's control, daily crucify them, and moment by moment draw on the Spirit's power to overcome them (see 2:20; 6:14).

• **5:25** God is interested in every part of our life, not just the spiritual part. As we live by the Holy Spirit's power, we need to submit every aspect of our life to God: emotional, physical, social, intellectual, vocational. Paul says that because we're saved, we should live like it! The Holy Spirit is the source of your new life, so keep in step with his leading. Don't let anything or anyone else determine your values and standards in any area of your life.

5:26 Everyone needs a certain amount of approval from others. But those who go out of their way to secure honors or to win popularity become conceited and show they are not following the Holy Spirit's leading. Those who look to God for approval won't need to envy others. Because we are God's sons and daughters, we have his Holy Spirit as the loving guarantee of his approval. Seek to please God, and the approval of others won't seem so important.

• **6:1-3** No Christian should ever think that he or she is totally independent and doesn't need help from others, and no one should feel excused from the task of helping others. The body of Christ—the church—functions only when the members work together for the common good. Do you know someone who needs help? Is there a Christian brother or sister who needs correction or encouragement? Humbly and gently reach out to that person offering to lift his or her load (John 13:34, 35).

6:4
2 Cor 13:5
6:6
1 Cor 9:11, 14
6:7
1 Cor 6:9
2 Cor 9:6
6:8
Job 4:8
Rom 8:13
6:9
2 Thes 3:13
6:10
Eph 2:19

⁴Pay careful attention to your own work, for then you will get the satisfaction of a job well done, and you won't need to compare yourself to anyone else. ⁵For we are each responsible for our own conduct.

⁶Those who are taught the word of God should provide for their teachers, sharing all good things with them.

⁷Don't be misled—you cannot mock the justice of God. You will always harvest what you plant. ⁸Those who live only to satisfy their own sinful nature will harvest decay and death from that sinful nature. But those who live to please the Spirit will harvest everlasting life from the Spirit. ⁹So let's not get tired of doing what is good. At just the right time we will reap a harvest of blessing if we don't give up. ¹⁰Therefore, whenever we have the opportunity, we should do good to everyone—especially to those in the family of faith.

Paul's Final Advice

6:11
1 Cor 16:21

¹¹Notice what large letters I use as I write these closing words in my own handwriting.

6:13
Rom 2:25

6:14
Rom 6:2, 6
1 Cor 2:2
Gal 2:20

¹²Those who are trying to force you to be circumcised want to look good to others. They don't want to be persecuted for teaching that the cross of Christ alone can save. ¹³And even those who advocate circumcision don't keep the whole law themselves. They only want you to be circumcised so they can boast about it and claim you as their disciples.

¹⁴As for me, may I never boast about anything except the cross of our Lord Jesus Christ. Because of that cross,* my interest in this world has been crucified, and the world's interest

6:14 Or *Because of him.*

OUR WRONG DESIRES VERSUS THE FRUIT OF THE SPIRIT The will of the Holy Spirit is in constant opposition to our sinful desires. The two are on opposite sides of the spiritual battle.	Our wrong desires are	The fruit of the Spirit is
	Evil	Good
	Destructive	Productive
	Easy to ignite	Difficult to ignite
	Difficult to stifle	Easy to stifle
	Self-centered	Self-giving
	Oppressive and possessive	Liberating and nurturing
	Decadent	Uplifting
	Sinful	Holy
	Deadly	Abundant life

• **6:4** When you do your very best, you feel good about the results. There is no need to compare yourself with others. People make comparisons for many reasons. Some point out others' flaws in order to feel better about themselves. Others simply want reassurance that they are doing well. When you are tempted to compare, look at Jesus Christ. His example will inspire you to do your very best, and his loving acceptance will comfort you when you fall short of your expectations.

• **6:6** Paul says that students should take care of the material needs of their teachers (1 Corinthians 9:7-12). It is easy to receive the benefit of good Bible teaching and then to take our spiritual leaders for granted, ignoring their financial and physical needs. We should care for our teachers, not grudgingly or reluctantly, but with a generous spirit, showing honor and appreciation for all they have done (1 Timothy 5:17, 18).

• **6:7, 8** It would certainly be a surprise if you planted corn and pumpkins came up. It's a natural law to harvest what we plant. It's true in other areas, too. If you gossip about your friends, you will lose their friendship. Every action has results. If you plant to please your own desires, you'll harvest a crop of sorrow and evil. If you plant to please God, you'll harvest joy and everlasting life. What kind of seeds are you planting?

6:9, 10 It is discouraging to continue to do right and receive no word of thanks or see no tangible results. But Paul challenged the Galatians, and he challenges us to keep on doing good and to trust God for the results. In due time, we will reap a harvest of blessing.

6:11 Up to this point, Paul had probably dictated the letter to a secretary. Here he takes the pen into his own hand to write his final, personal greetings. Paul did this in other letters as well, to add emphasis to his words and to validate that the letter was genuine.

6:13 Some of the Judaizers were emphasizing circumcision as proof of holiness, but were ignoring the other Jewish laws. People often choose a certain principle or prohibition and make it the measure of faith. Some may condemn drunkenness but ignore gluttony. Others may despise promiscuity but tolerate prejudice. Some who are adamant against homosexuality ignore child abuse. The Bible in its entirety is our rule of faith and practice. We cannot pick and choose the mandates we will follow.

• **6:14** The world is full of enticements. Daily we are confronted with subtle cultural pressures and overt propaganda. The only way to escape these destructive influences is to ask God to help crucify our interest in them, just as Paul did. How much do the interests of this world matter to you? (See 2:20 and 5:24 for more on this concept.)

in me has also died. ¹⁵It doesn't matter whether we have been circumcised or not. What counts is whether we have been transformed into a new creation. ¹⁶May God's peace and mercy be upon all who live by this principle; they are the new people of God.*

¹⁷From now on, don't let anyone trouble me with these things. For I bear on my body the scars that show I belong to Jesus.

¹⁸Dear brothers and sisters,* may the grace of our Lord Jesus Christ be with your spirit. Amen.

6:16 Greek *this principle, and upon the Israel of God.*   **6:18** Greek *Brothers.*

6:15
1 Cor 7:19
2 Cor 5:17
Gal 5:6

6:17
2 Cor 1:5; 4:10

6:18
Rom 16:20
2 Tim 4:22

• **6:15** It is easy to get caught up with the externals. Beware of those who emphasize actions that we should or shouldn't do, with no concern for the inward condition of the heart. Living a good life without an inward change leads to a shallow or empty spiritual walk. What matters to God is that we be completely changed from the inside out (2 Corinthians 5:17).

• **6:18** Paul's letter to the Galatians boldly declares the freedom of the Christian. Doubtless these early Christians in Galatia wanted to grow in the Christian life, but they were being misled by those who said this could be done only by keeping certain Jewish laws.

How strange it would be for a prisoner who had been set free to walk back into his or her cell and refuse to leave! How strange for an animal, released from a trap, to go back inside it! How sad for a believer to be freed from the bondage of sin, only to return to rigid conformity to a set of rules and regulations!

If you believe in Jesus Christ, you have been set free. Instead of going back into some form of slavery, whether to legalism or to sin, use your freedom to live for Christ and serve him as he desires.

EPHESIANS

EPHESIANS

OUR churches come in all styles and shapes—secret meetings in homes; wide-open gatherings in amphitheaters; worship services packing thousands into a sanctuary while an overflow crowd watches on closed-circuit television; handfuls who kneel in urban storefronts. Buildings will vary, but the church is not confined to four walls. The church of Jesus Christ is *people*, his people, of every race and nation, who love Christ and are committed to serving him.

The "church age" began at Pentecost (Acts 2). Born in Jerusalem, the church spread rapidly through the ministry of the apostles and the early believers. Fanned by persecution, the gospel flame then spread to other cities and nations. On three courageous journeys, Paul and his associates established local assemblies in scores of Gentile cities.

One of the most prominent of those churches was at Ephesus. It was established in A.D. 53 on Paul's homeward journey to Jerusalem. But Paul returned a year later, on his third missionary trip, and stayed there for three years, preaching and teaching with great effectiveness (Acts 19:1–20). At another time, Paul met with the Ephesian elders, and he sent Timothy to serve as their leader (1 Timothy 1:3). Just a few years later, Paul was sent as a prisoner to Rome. There, he was visited by messengers from various churches, including Tychicus of Ephesus. Paul wrote this letter to the church and sent it with Tychicus. Not written to counteract heresy or to confront any specific problem, Ephesians is a letter of encouragement. In it Paul describes the nature and appearance of the church, and he challenges believers to function as the living body of Christ on earth.

After a warm greeting (1:1, 2), Paul affirms the nature of the church—the glorious fact that believers in Christ have been showered with God's kindness (1:3–8), chosen for greatness (1:9–12), marked with the Holy Spirit (1:13, 14), filled with the Spirit's power (1:15–23), freed from sin's curse and bondage (2:1–10), and brought near to God (2:11–18). As part of God's "house," we stand with the prophets, apostles, Jews, Gentiles, and Christ himself (2:19—3:13). Then, as though overcome with emotion by remembering all that God has done, Paul challenges the Ephesians to live close to Christ, and he breaks into spontaneous praise (3:14–21).

Paul then turns his attention to the implications of being in the body of Christ, the church. Believers should have unity in their commitment to Christ and their use of spiritual gifts (4:1–16). They should have the highest moral standards (4:17—6:9). For the individual, this means rejecting pagan practices (4:17—5:20), and for the family, this means mutual submission and love (5:21—6:9).

Paul then reminds believers that the church is in a constant battle with the forces of darkness and that they should use every spiritual weapon at their disposal (6:10–17). He concludes by asking for their prayers, commissioning Tychicus, and giving a benediction (6:18–24).

As you read this masterful description of the church, thank God for the diversity and unity in his family, pray for your brothers and sisters across the world, and draw close to those in your local church.

VITAL STATISTICS

PURPOSE:
To strengthen the believers in Ephesus in their Christian faith by explaining the nature and purpose of the church, the body of Christ

AUTHOR:
Paul

ORIGINAL AUDIENCE:
The church at Ephesus, then circulated to neighboring local churches

DATE WRITTEN:
Approximately A.D. 60, from Rome, during Paul's imprisonment there

SETTING:
The letter was not written to confront any heresy or problem in the churches. It was sent with Tychicus to strengthen and encourage the churches in the area. Paul had spent over three years with the Ephesian church. As a result, he was very close to them. Paul met with the elders of the Ephesian church at Miletus (Acts 20:17–38)—a meeting that was filled with great sadness because he was leaving them for what he thought would be the last time. Because the letter contains no specific references to people or problems in the Ephesian church and because the words "in Ephesus" (1:1) are not present in some early manuscripts, Paul may have intended this to be a circular letter to be read to all the churches in the area.

KEY VERSES:
"For there is one body and one Spirit, just as you have been called to one glorious hope for the future. There is one Lord, one faith, one baptism, and one God and Father, who is over all and in all and living through all" (4:4–6).

KEY PEOPLE:
Paul, Tychicus

THE BLUEPRINT

1. Unity in Christ
   (1:1—3:21)
2. Unity in the body of Christ
   (4:1— 6:24)

In this letter, Paul explains the wonderful things that we have received through Christ and refers to the church as a body to illustrate unity of purpose and show how each individual member is a part that must work together with all the other parts. In our own life, we should work to eradicate all backbiting, gossip, criticism, jealousy, anger, and bitterness, because these are barriers to unity in the church.

MEGATHEMES

THEME	EXPLANATION	IMPORTANCE
God's Purpose	According to God's eternal, loving plan, he directs, carries out, and sustains our salvation.	When we respond to Christ's love by trusting in him, his purpose becomes our mission. Have you committed yourself to fulfilling God's purpose?
Christ the Center	Christ is exalted as the center of the universe and the focus of history. He is the head of the body, the church. He is the Creator and sustainer of all creation.	Because Christ is central to everything, his power must be central in us. Begin by placing all your priorities under his control.
Living Church	Paul describes the nature of the church. The church, under Christ's control, is a living body, a family, a dwelling. God gives believers special abilities by his Holy Spirit to build the church.	We are part of Christ's body, and we must live in vital union with him. Our conduct must be consistent with this living relation-ship. Use your God-given abilities to equip believers for service. Fulfill your role in the living church.
New Family	Because God through Christ paid our penalty for sin and forgave us, we have been reconciled— brought near to him. We are a new society, a new family. Being united with Christ means we are to treat one another as family members.	We are one family in Christ, so there should be no barriers, no divisions, no basis for discrimination. We all belong to him, so we should live in harmony with one another.
Christian Conduct	Paul encourages all Christians to wise, dynamic Christian living, for with privileges goes family responsibility. As a new community, we are to live by Christ's new standards.	God provides his Holy Spirit to enable us to live his way. To utilize the Spirit's power, we must lay aside our evil desires and draw on the power of his new life. Submit your will to Christ, and seek to love others.

1. Unity in Christ

Greetings from Paul

1 This letter is from Paul, chosen by the will of God to be an apostle of Christ Jesus.
I am writing to God's holy people in Ephesus,* who are faithful followers of Christ Jesus.
²May God our Father and the Lord Jesus Christ give you grace and peace.

1:2
Rom 1:7
Titus 1:4

1:1 The most ancient manuscripts do not include *in Ephesus.*

• **1:1** Paul wrote this letter to the Ephesian believers and all other believers to give them in-depth teaching about how to nurture and maintain the unity of the church. He wanted to put this important information in written form because he was in prison for preach-ing the Good News and could not visit the churches himself. The words "in Ephesus" are not present in some early manuscripts. Therefore, this was very likely a circular letter. It was first sent to Ephesus and then circulated to neighboring local churches. Paul mentions no particular problems or local situations, and he offers no personal greetings.

1:1 Paul had been a Christian for nearly 30 years. He had taken three missionary trips and established churches all around the Mediterranean Sea. When he wrote Ephesians, Paul was under house arrest in Rome (see Acts 28:16ff). Though a prisoner, he was free to have visitors and write letters. For more information on Paul, see his Profile in Acts 9, p. 1837.

• **1:1** Ephesus was one of the five major cities in the Roman Empire, along with Rome, Corinth, Antioch, and Alexandria. Paul first visited Ephesus on his second missionary journey (Acts 18:19-21). During his third missionary journey, he stayed there for almost three years (Acts 19). Paul later met again with the elders of the Ephesian church at Miletus (Acts 20:16-38). Ephesus was a commercial, political, and religious center for all of Asia Minor. The temple to the Greek goddess Artemis (Diana is her Roman equivalent) was located there.

1:1 "Faithful followers of Christ Jesus"—what an excellent repu-tation! Such a label would be an honor for any believer. What would it take for others to characterize you as a faithful follower of Christ Jesus? Hold fast to your faith, one day at a time; faith-fully obey God, even in the details of life. Then, like the Ephesians, you will be known as a person who is faithful to the Lord.

1:4
2 Thes 2:13
1 Pet 1:2, 20

1:5
Rom 8:15, 29

1:6
Rom 3:24
Col 1:13

1:7
Col 1:14
Heb 9:12

Spiritual Blessings

³All praise to God, the Father of our Lord Jesus Christ, who has blessed us with every spiritual blessing in the heavenly realms because we are united with Christ. ⁴Even before he made the world, God loved us and chose us in Christ to be holy and without fault in his eyes. ⁵God decided in advance to adopt us into his own family by bringing us to himself through Jesus Christ. This is what he wanted to do, and it gave him great pleasure. ⁶So we praise God for the glorious grace he has poured out on us who belong to his dear Son.* ⁷He is so rich in

1:6 Greek *to us in the beloved.*

LOCATION OF EPHESUS
Ephesus was a strategic city, ranking in importance with Alexandria in Egypt and Antioch of Syria as a port. It lay on the most western edge of Asia Minor (modern-day Turkey), the most important port on the Aegean Sea on the main route from Rome to the east.

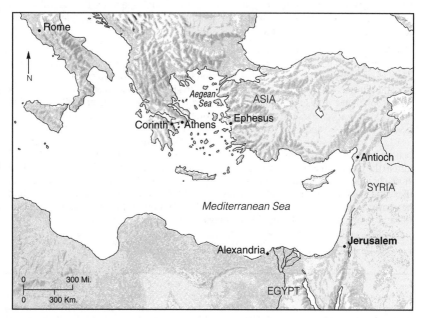

- **1:3** "Who has blessed us with every spiritual blessing in the heavenly realms" means that in Christ we have all the benefits of knowing God—being chosen for salvation, being adopted as his children, forgiveness, insight, the gifts of the Spirit, power to do God's will, the hope of living forever with Christ. Because we have an intimate relationship with Christ, we can enjoy these blessings now. The "heavenly realms" means that these blessings are eternal, not temporal. The blessings come from Christ's spiritual realm, not the earthly realm of the goddess Artemis. Other references to the heavenly realms in this letter include 1:20; 2:6; 3:10. Such passages reveal Christ in his victorious, exalted role as ruler of all.

- **1:4** Paul says that God "chose us" to emphasize that salvation depends totally on God. We are not saved because we deserve it but because God is gracious and freely gives salvation. We did not influence God's decision to save us; he saved us according to his plan. Thus, there is no way to take credit for our salvation or to allow room for pride. The mystery of salvation originated in the timeless mind of God long before we existed. It is hard to understand how God could accept us. But because of Christ, we are holy and blameless in his sight. God chose us, and when we belong to him through Jesus Christ, God looks at us as if we had never sinned. All we can do is express our thanks for his wonderful love.

1:5 That God "decided in advance to adopt us" is another way of saying that salvation is God's work and not our own doing. In his infinite love, God has adopted us as his own children. Through

Jesus' sacrifice, he has brought us into his family and made us heirs along with Jesus (Romans 8:17). In Roman law, adopted children had the same rights and privileges as biological children, even if they had been slaves. Paul uses this term to show how strong our relationship to God is. Have you entered into this loving relationship with God? For more on the meaning of adoption, see Galatians 4:5-7.

1:7 To speak of Jesus' blood was an important first-century way of speaking of Christ's death. His death points to two wonderful truths—redemption and forgiveness. *Redemption* was the price paid to gain freedom for a slave (Leviticus 25:47-54). Through his death, Jesus paid the price to release us from slavery to sin. *Forgiveness* was granted in Old Testament times on the basis of the shedding of animals' blood (Leviticus 17:11). Now we are forgiven on the basis of the shedding of Jesus' blood—he died as the perfect and final sacrifice (see also Romans 5:9; Ephesians 2:13; Colossians 1:20; Hebrews 9:22; 1 Peter 1:19).

- **1:7, 8** God showered his kindness on us—this is also called God's "grace." This is his voluntary and loving favor given to those he saves. We can't earn salvation, nor do we deserve it. No religious, intellectual, or moral effort can gain it, because it comes only from God's mercy and love. Without God's grace, no person can be saved. To receive it, we must acknowledge that we cannot save ourselves, that only God can save us, and that our only way to receive this loving favor is through faith in Christ.

kindness and grace that he purchased our freedom with the blood of his Son and forgave our sins. ⁸He has showered his kindness on us, along with all wisdom and understanding.

⁹God has now revealed to us his mysterious plan regarding Christ, a plan to fulfill his own good pleasure. ¹⁰And this is the plan: At the right time he will bring everything together under the authority of Christ—everything in heaven and on earth. ¹¹Furthermore, because we are united with Christ, we have received an inheritance from God,* for he chose us in advance, and he makes everything work out according to his plan.

¹²God's purpose was that we Jews who were the first to trust in Christ would bring praise and glory to God. ¹³And now you Gentiles have also heard the truth, the Good News that God saves you. And when you believed in Christ, he identified you as his own* by giving you the Holy Spirit, whom he promised long ago. ¹⁴The Spirit is God's guarantee that he will give us the inheritance he promised and that he has purchased us to be his own people. He did this so we would praise and glorify him.

Paul's Prayer for Spiritual Wisdom

¹⁵Ever since I first heard of your strong faith in the Lord Jesus and your love for God's people everywhere,* ¹⁶I have not stopped thanking God for you. I pray for you constantly, ¹⁷asking God, the glorious Father of our Lord Jesus Christ, to give you spiritual wisdom* and insight so that you might grow in your knowledge of God. ¹⁸I pray that your hearts will be flooded with light so that you can understand the confident hope he has given to those he called— his holy people who are his rich and glorious inheritance.*

¹⁹I also pray that you will understand the incredible greatness of God's power for us who believe him. This is the same mighty power ²⁰that raised Christ from the dead and seated him in the place of honor at God's right hand in the heavenly realms. ²¹Now he is far above any ruler or authority or power or leader or anything else—not only in this world but also in the world to come. ²²God has put all things under the authority of Christ and has made him head over all things for the benefit of the church. ²³And the church is his body; it is made full and complete by Christ, who fills all things everywhere with himself.

1:11 Or *we have become God's inheritance.*   **1:13** Or *he put his seal on you.*   **1:15** Some manuscripts read *your faithfulness to the Lord Jesus and to God's people everywhere.*   **1:17** Or *to give you the Spirit of wisdom.*   **1:18** Or *called, and the rich and glorious inheritance he has given to his holy people.*

1:9
Rom 16:25
Eph 3:3, 9

1:10
Mark 1:15
Gal 4:4
Col 1:16, 20

1:11
Rom 8:28-29
Eph 3:11

1:12
Eph 1:6, 14

1:13
2 Cor 1:22
Eph 4:30
Col 1:5

1:14
Rom 8:23
2 Cor 1:22; 5:5

1:16
Col 1:9

1:17
1 Cor 2:9-12

1:18
Acts 26:18
Eph 1:11; 4:4

1:19
Eph 3:7, 16; 6:10
Phil 3:21

1:20
Acts 2:24

1:21
Phil 2:9
Col 1:16; 2:10

1:22
Eph 4:15
Col 1:18; 2:19

1:23
Eph 3:19; 4:10
Col 1:19; 3:11

1:9, 10 God was not intentionally keeping his mysterious plan a secret, but his plan for the world could not be fully understood until Christ rose from the dead. His purpose for sending Christ was to unite Jews and Gentiles in one body with Christ as the head. Many people still do not understand God's plan; but at the right time, he will bring us together to be with him forever. Then everyone will understand. On that day, all people will bow to Jesus as Lord, either because they love him or because they fear his power (see Philippians 2:10, 11).

- **1:11** God's purpose is to offer salvation to the world, just as he planned to do long ago. God is sovereign; he is in charge. When your life seems chaotic, rest in this truth: Jesus is Lord, and God is in control. God's purpose to save you cannot be thwarted, no matter what evil Satan may bring.

- **1:13, 14** The Holy Spirit is God's guarantee that we belong to him and that he will do what he has promised. The Holy Spirit is like a down payment, a deposit, a validating signature on the contract. The presence of the Holy Spirit in us demonstrates the genuineness of our faith, proves that we are God's children, and secures eternal life for us. His power works in us to transform us now, and what we experience now is a taste of the total change we will experience in eternity.

- **1:16, 17** Paul prayed for the believers to know God better. How do you get to know someone? By reading biographical information or historical data about him? That will help you know a lot *about* that person, but it won't enable you to actually *know* him. If you want to get to know someone, you have to spend time with that person; there is no shortcut. The same holds true with God. Reading the Bible, great works of theology, and devotional material is wonderful, but there is no substitute for knowing God

personally. What about you? Do you really *know* God, or do you just know *about* him? The difference is in spending time with him. Study Jesus' life in the Gospels to see what he was like on earth two thousand years ago, and get to know him in prayer now. Personal knowledge of Christ will change your life.

1:19, 20 The world fears the power of the atom, yet we belong to the God of the universe, who not only created that atomic power but also raised Jesus Christ from the dead. God's incomparably great power is available to help you. There is nothing too difficult for him.

- **1:20-22** Having been raised from the dead, Christ is now the head of the church, the ultimate authority over the world. Jesus is the Messiah, God's anointed one, the one Israel longed for, the one who would set their broken world right. As Christians we can be confident that God has won the final victory and is in control of everything. We need not fear any dictator or nation or even death or Satan himself. The contract has been signed and sealed; we are waiting just a short while for delivery. Paul says, in Romans 8:37-39, that nothing can separate us from God and his love.

- **1:22, 23** Christ fills the church with gifts and blessings. The church should be the full expression of Christ, who himself fills everything (see 3:19). When reading Ephesians, it is important to remember that it was written primarily to the entire church, not merely to an individual. Christ is the head, and we are the body of his church (Paul uses this metaphor in Romans 12:4, 5; 1 Corinthians 12:12-27; and Colossians 3:15 as well as throughout the book of Ephesians). The image of the body shows the church's unity. Each member is involved with all the others as they go about doing Christ's work on earth. We should not attempt to work, serve, or worship merely on our own. We need the entire body.

Made Alive with Christ

2:1
Eph 2:5
Col 2:13

2:3
Gal 5:24
Col 3:6

2:5
Rom 5:6; 6:4
Eph 2:1
Col 2:13

2 Once you were dead because of your disobedience and your many sins. ²You used to live in sin, just like the rest of the world, obeying the devil—the commander of the powers in the unseen world.* He is the spirit at work in the hearts of those who refuse to obey God. ³All of us used to live that way, following the passionate desires and inclinations of our sinful nature. By our very nature we were subject to God's anger, just like everyone else.

⁴But God is so rich in mercy, and he loved us so much, ⁵that even though we were dead

2:2 Greek *obeying the commander of the power of the air.*

OUR TRUE IDENTITY IN CHRIST

Romans 3:24 . . . . We are justified (declared "righteous").

Romans 8:1 . . . . No condemnation awaits us.

Romans 8:2 . . . . We are set free from the power of sin that leads to death.

1 Corinthians 1:2 . . . . We are sanctified (made holy) in Jesus Christ.

1 Corinthians 1:30 . . . . . . We are pure and holy in Christ.

1 Corinthians 15:22 . . . . . We will be given new life at the resurrection.

2 Corinthians 5:17 . . . . . . We are new persons.

2 Corinthians 5:21 . . . . . . We are made right with God.

Galatians 3:28 . . . . We are one in Christ with all other believers.

Ephesians 1:3 . . . . We are blessed with every spiritual blessing in Christ.

Ephesians 1:4 . . . . We are holy and without fault.

Ephesians 1:5, 6 . . . . We are adopted as God's children.

Ephesians 1:7 . . . . Our sins are taken away, and we are forgiven.

Ephesians 1:10, 11 . . . . . We will be brought under Christ's authority.

Ephesians 1:13 . . . . We are identified as belonging to God by the Holy Spirit.

Ephesians 2:6 . . . . We have been raised up to sit with Christ in the heavenly realms.

Ephesians 2:10 . . . . We are God's masterpiece.

Ephesians 2:13 . . . . We have been brought near to God.

Ephesians 3:6 . . . . We share in the promise of blessings through Christ.

Ephesians 3:12 . . . . We can come boldly and confidently into God's presence.

Ephesians 5:29, 30 . . . . . We are members of Christ's body, the church.

Colossians 2:10 . . . . We are made complete in Christ.

Colossians 2:11 . . . . We are set free from our sinful nature.

2 Timothy 2:10 . . . . We will have eternal glory.

2:1, 2 Immediately after his prayer, Paul reminds the Ephesians of the reality of personal sin. Like them, we must never forget our past, the condition from which Jesus saved us. Those memories are the best fuel for our gratitude to Christ for all he has done in our behalf.

2:2 Paul describes Satan, the devil, as "the commander of the powers in the unseen world." Paul's readers believed that Satan and the evil spiritual forces inhabited the region between earth and sky. Satan is thus pictured as ruling an evil spiritual kingdom—the demons and those who are against Christ. In the resurrection, Christ was victorious over the devil and his power. Therefore, Jesus Christ is the permanent ruler of the whole world; the devil is only the temporary ruler of the part of the world that chooses to follow him.

• **2:3** The fact that all people, without exception, commit sin proves that without Christ we have a sinful nature. We are lost in sin and cannot save ourselves. Does this mean only Christians do good? Of course not—many people do good to others. On a relative scale, many are moral, kind, and law abiding. Comparing these people to criminals, we would say that they are very good indeed. But on God's absolute scale, *no one* is good enough to earn salvation ("dead because of your disobedience and your many sins," 2:1). Only through being united with Christ's perfect life can we become good in God's sight. "Subject to God's anger"

refers to those who are to receive God's wrath because of their rejection of Christ.

2:4 We were dead in our sins, *but God* . . . We were rebels against him, *but God* . . . We were enslaved by the devil and our sinful natures, *but God* . . . These may be the two most welcome words in all of Scripture: "but God." God could have left us spiritually dead, in rebellion against him and in bondage to our sins. *But he didn't.* He did not save us because of, but rather in spite of, what he saw in us. In addition to thanking him for what he has done for us, we should also show humble patience and tolerance for others who seem unworthy or undeserving of our love and compassion. They may be spiritually dull, rebellious, and even antagonistic toward God. So were we; *but God loved us anyway.* Can we do less for fellow sinners?

• **2:4, 5** In the previous verses Paul wrote about our old sinful nature (2:1-3). Here Paul emphasizes that we do not need to live any longer under sin's power. The penalty of sin and its power over us were miraculously destroyed by Christ on the cross. Through faith in Christ we stand acquitted, or not guilty, before God (Romans 3:21, 22). God does not take us out of the world or make us robots—we will still feel like sinning, and sometimes we will sin. The difference is that before we became Christians, we were dead in sin and were slaves to our sinful nature. But now we are alive with Christ (see also Galatians 2:20).

because of our sins, he gave us life when he raised Christ from the dead. (It is only by God's grace that you have been saved!) 6For he raised us from the dead along with Christ and seated us with him in the heavenly realms because we are united with Christ Jesus. 7So God can point to us in all future ages as examples of the incredible wealth of his grace and kindness toward us, as shown in all he has done for us who are united with Christ Jesus.

2:7
Titus 3:4

8God saved you by his grace when you believed. And you can't take credit for this; it is a gift from God. 9Salvation is not a reward for the good things we have done, so none of us can boast about it. 10For we are God's masterpiece. He has created us anew in Christ Jesus, so we can do the good things he planned for us long ago.

2:8
John 4:10
2:9
Rom 3:28
2 Tim 1:9
Titus 3:5

Oneness and Peace in Christ

11Don't forget that you Gentiles used to be outsiders. You were called "uncircumcised heathens" by the Jews, who were proud of their circumcision, even though it affected only their bodies and not their hearts. 12In those days you were living apart from Christ. You were excluded from citizenship among the people of Israel, and you did not know the covenant promises God had made to them. You lived in this world without God and without hope. 13But now you have been united with Christ Jesus. Once you were far away from God, but now you have been brought near to him through the blood of Christ.

2:11
Col 2:11
2:12
Rom 9:4
1 Thes 4:13
2:13
Col 1:20
2:14
1 Cor 12:13

14For Christ himself has brought peace to us. He united Jews and Gentiles into one people when, in his own body on the cross, he broke down the wall of hostility that separated us. 15He did this by ending the system of law with its commandments and regulations. He made peace between Jews and Gentiles by creating in himself one new people from the two groups. 16Together as one body, Christ reconciled both groups to God by means of his death on the cross, and our hostility toward each other was put to death.

2:15
2 Cor 5:17
Gal 3:28
Col 1:21-22; 2:14
2:16
Col 1:20
2:17
Isa 57:19
Zech 9:10

17He brought this Good News of peace to you Gentiles who were far away from him, and peace to the Jews who were near. 18Now all of us can come to the Father through the same Holy Spirit because of what Christ has done for us.

2:18
Eph 3:12; 4:4

2:6 Because of Christ's resurrection, we know that our body will also be raised from the dead (1 Corinthians 15:2-23) and that we have been given the power to live as Christians now (1:19). These ideas are combined in Paul's image of sitting with Christ in "the heavenly realms" (see the note on 1:3). Our eternal life with Christ is certain because we are united in his powerful victory.

· **2:8, 9** When someone gives you a gift, do you say, "That's very nice—now how much do I owe you?" No, the appropriate response to a gift is "Thank you." Yet how often Christians, even after they have been given the gift of salvation, feel obligated to try to work their way to God. Because our salvation and even our faith are gifts, we should respond with gratitude, praise, and joy.

· **2:8-10** We become Christians through God's unmerited favor, not as the result of any effort, ability, intelligent choice, or act of service on our part. However, out of gratitude for this free gift, we will seek to help and serve others with kindness, love, and gentleness, and not merely to please ourselves. While no action or work we do can help us obtain salvation, God's intention is that our salvation will result in acts of service. We are not saved merely for our own benefit but to serve Christ and build up the church (4:12).

2:10 We are God's masterpiece (work of art, workmanship). Our salvation is something only God can do. It is his powerful, creative work in us. If God considers us his masterpieces, we dare not treat ourselves or others with disrespect or as inferior work.

· **2:11-13** Pious Jews considered all non-Jews (Gentiles) ceremonially unclean. They thought of themselves as pure and clean because of their national heritage and religious ceremonies. Paul pointed out that Jews and Gentiles alike were unclean before God and needed to be cleansed by Christ. In order to realize how great a gift salvation is, we need to remember our former natural, unclean condition. Have you ever felt separate, excluded, hopeless? These verses are for you. No one is alienated from Christ's love or from the body of believers.

2:11-13 Jews and Gentiles alike could be guilty of spiritual pride—Jews for thinking their faith and traditions elevated them above everyone else, Gentiles for trusting in their achievements,

power, or position. Spiritual pride blinds us to our own faults and magnifies the faults of others. Be careful not to become proud of your salvation. Instead, humbly thank God for what he has done, and encourage others who might be struggling in their faith.

· **2:11-16** Before Christ's coming, Gentiles and Jews kept apart from one another. Jews considered Gentiles beyond God's saving power and therefore without hope. Gentiles resented Jewish claims. Christ revealed the total sinfulness of both Jews and Gentiles, and then he offered his salvation to both. Only Christ breaks down the walls of prejudice, reconciles all believers to God, and unifies us in one body.

· **2:14ff** Christ has destroyed the barriers people build between themselves. Because these walls have been removed, we can have real unity with people who are not like us. This is true reconciliation. Because of Christ's death, we are all one (2:14); our hostility against each other has been put to death (2:16); we can all have access to the Father by the Holy Spirit (2:18); we are no longer strangers or foreigners to God (2:19); and we are all being built into a holy temple with Christ as our chief cornerstone (2:20, 21).

· **2:14-22** There are many barriers that can divide us from other Christians: age, appearance, intelligence, political persuasion, economic status, race, theological perspective. One of the best ways to stifle Christ's love is to be friendly with only those people that we like. Fortunately, Christ has knocked down the barriers and has unified all believers in one family. His cross should be the focus of our unity. The Holy Spirit helps us look beyond the barriers to the unity we are called to enjoy.

2:15 By his death, Christ ended the angry resentment between Jews and Gentiles, caused by the Jewish laws that favored the Jews and excluded the Gentiles. Christ died to abolish that whole system of Jewish laws. Then he took the two groups that had been opposed to each other and made them parts of himself. "One new people" means that Christ made a single entity out of the two. Thus, he fused all believers together to become one in himself.

2:17, 18 The Jews were near to God because they already knew of him through the Scriptures and worshiped him in their religious

2:20
Isa 28:16
Matt 16:18
Acts 4:11
1 Cor 3:11
1 Pet 2:4-8
Rev 21:14

2:21
1 Cor 3:16
Eph 4:15-16

3:1
Eph 4:1
2 Tim 1:8

3:2
Col 1:25

3:3
Eph 1:9-10
Col 1:26

3:5
Eph 1:17

3:6
Eph 2:14-16

3:7
Rom 15:18
Col 1:23, 25

3:8
1 Cor 15:9-10

3:9
Rom 16:25

A Temple for the Lord

¹⁹So now you Gentiles are no longer strangers and foreigners. You are citizens along with all of God's holy people. You are members of God's family. ²⁰Together, we are his house, built on the foundation of the apostles and the prophets. And the cornerstone is Christ Jesus himself. ²¹We are carefully joined together in him, becoming a holy temple for the Lord. ²²Through him you Gentiles are also being made part of this dwelling where God lives by his Spirit.

God's Mysterious Plan Revealed

3 When I think of all this, I, Paul, a prisoner of Christ Jesus for the benefit of you Gentiles* . . . ²assuming, by the way, that you know God gave me the special responsibility of extending his grace to you Gentiles. ³As I briefly wrote earlier, God himself revealed his mysterious plan to me. ⁴As you read what I have written, you will understand my insight into this plan regarding Christ. ⁵God did not reveal it to previous generations, but now by his Spirit he has revealed it to his holy apostles and prophets.

⁶And this is God's plan: Both Gentiles and Jews who believe the Good News share equally in the riches inherited by God's children. Both are part of the same body, and both enjoy the promise of blessings because they belong to Christ Jesus.* ⁷By God's grace and mighty power, I have been given the privilege of serving him by spreading this Good News.

⁸Though I am the least deserving of all God's people, he graciously gave me the privilege of telling the Gentiles about the endless treasures available to them in Christ. ⁹I was chosen

3:1 Paul resumes this thought in verse 14: "When I think of all this, I fall to my knees and pray to the Father."
3:6 Or *because they are united with Christ Jesus.*

OUR LIVES BEFORE AND AFTER CHRIST

Before	After
Dead because of sin	Made alive with Christ
Under God's anger	Shown God's mercy and given salvation
Followed the ways of the world	Stand for Christ and truth
God's enemies	God's children
Enslaved to the devil	Free in Christ to love, serve, and sit with him
Followed our evil thoughts and desires	Raised up with Christ to glory

---

ceremonies. The Gentiles were far away because they knew little or nothing about God. Because neither group could be saved by good deeds, knowledge, or sincerity, both needed to hear about the salvation available through Jesus Christ. Both Jews and Gentiles are now free to come to God through Christ. You have been brought near to him (2:13).

• **2:19-22** A church building is sometimes called God's house. In reality, God's household is not a building but a group of people. He lives in us and shows himself to a watching world through us. People can see that God is love and that Christ is Lord as we live in harmony with each other and in accordance with what God says in his Word. We are citizens of God's Kingdom and members of his household.

2:20 What does it mean to be built on the foundation of the apostles and prophets? It means that the church is not built on modern ideas but rather on the spiritual heritage given to us by the early apostles and prophets of the Christian church.

3:1 Paul was under house arrest in Rome for preaching about Christ. The religious leaders in Jerusalem, who felt threatened by Christ's teachings and didn't believe he was the Messiah, pressured the Romans to arrest Paul and bring him to trial for treason and for causing rebellion among the Jews. Paul had appealed for his case to be heard by the emperor, and he was awaiting trial (see Acts 28:16-31). Even though he was under arrest, Paul maintained his firm belief that God was in control of all that happened to him. Do circumstances make you wonder if God has lost control of this world? Like Paul, remember that no matter what happens, God directs the world's affairs.

3:2, 3 Paul's "special responsibility" refers to the special stewardship, trust, or commitment that Paul had been given. He had

been assigned the special work of preaching the Good News to the Gentiles, God's great plan shown to Paul in a revelation.

• **3:5, 6** God's plan was not revealed to previous generations, not because God wanted to keep something from his people, but because he would reveal it to everyone in his perfect timing. God planned to have Jews and Gentiles comprise one body, the church. It was known in the Old Testament that the Gentiles would receive salvation (Isaiah 49:6); but it was never revealed in the Old Testament that all Gentile and Jewish believers would become equal in the body of Christ. Yet this equality was accomplished when Jesus destroyed the "wall of hostility" and created "one new people" (2:14, 15).

• **3:7** When Paul became a servant of the gospel, God gave him the ability to share the gospel of Christ effectively. You are not an apostle, and you may not be an evangelist, but God will give you opportunities to tell others about Christ. And with the opportunities he will provide the ability, courage, and power. Make yourself available to God as his servant whenever an opportunity presents itself. As you focus on the other person and his or her needs, God will communicate your caring attitude. Your words will be natural, loving, and compelling.

3:8 When Paul describes himself as "the least deserving of all God's people," he means that without God's help, he would never be able to do God's work. Yet God chose him to share the Good News with the Gentiles and gave him the power to do it. If we feel that our role is minor, we may be right—except that we have forgotten what a difference God makes. How does God want to use you? Draw on his power, do your part, and faithfully perform the special role God has called you to play in his plan.

to explain to everyone* this mysterious plan that God, the Creator of all things, had kept secret from the beginning.

¹⁰God's purpose in all this was to use the church to display his wisdom in its rich variety to all the unseen rulers and authorities in the heavenly places. ¹¹This was his eternal plan, which he carried out through Christ Jesus our Lord.

¹²Because of Christ and our faith in him,* we can now come boldly and confidently into God's presence. ¹³So please don't lose heart because of my trials here. I am suffering for you, so you should feel honored.

Paul's Prayer for Spiritual Growth

¹⁴When I think of all this, I fall to my knees and pray to the Father,* ¹⁵the Creator of everything in heaven and on earth.* ¹⁶I pray that from his glorious, unlimited resources he will empower you with inner strength through his Spirit. ¹⁷Then Christ will make his home in your hearts as you trust in him. Your roots will grow down into God's love and keep you strong. ¹⁸And may you have the power to understand, as all God's people should, how wide, how long, how high, and how deep his love is. ¹⁹May you experience the love of Christ, though it is too great to understand fully. Then you will be made complete with all the fullness of life and power that comes from God.

²⁰Now all glory to God, who is able, through his mighty power at work within us, to accomplish infinitely more than we might ask or think. ²¹Glory to him in the church and in Christ Jesus through all generations forever and ever! Amen.

2. Unity in the body of Christ

4 Therefore I, a prisoner for serving the Lord, beg you to lead a life worthy of your calling, for you have been called by God. ²Always be humble and gentle. Be patient with each

3:10 Rom 11:33; 1 Cor 2:7; Eph 1:21; 6:12; 1 Pet 1:12
3:11 Eph 1:11
3:12 Eph 2:18; Heb 4:16
3:14 Phil 2:10
3:16 Phil 4:13, 19; Col 1:11
3:17 John 14:23; Col 2:7
3:18 John 1:16; Col 2:9-10
3:19 Col 2:10
3:20 Eph 1:19-20; Col 1:29
4:1 Eph 3:1; Phil 1:7, 13
4:2 Col 3:12-13

3:9 Some manuscripts do not include *to everyone.*   **3:12** Or *Because of Christ's faithfulness.*   **3:14** Some manuscripts read *the Father of our Lord Jesus Christ.*   **3:15** Or *from whom every family in heaven and on earth takes its name.*

3:10 The "rulers and authorities in the heavenly places" are either angels who are witnesses to these events (see 1 Peter 1:12), or hostile spiritual forces opposed to God (2:2; 6:12).

3:12 It is an awesome privilege to be able to approach God with freedom and confidence. Most of us would be apprehensive in the presence of a powerful ruler. But thanks to Christ, by faith we can enter directly into God's presence through prayer. We know we'll be welcomed with open arms because we are God's children through our union with Christ. Don't be afraid of God. Talk with him about everything. He is waiting to hear from you.

3:13 Why should Paul's suffering make the Ephesians feel honored? If Paul had not preached the Good News, he would not be in jail—but then the Ephesians would not have heard the Good News and been converted either. Just as a mother endures the pain of childbirth in order to bring new life into the world, Paul endured the pain of persecution in order to bring new believers to Christ. Obeying Christ is never easy. He calls you to take your cross and follow him (Matthew 16:24)—that is, to be willing to endure pain so that God's message of salvation can reach the entire world. We should feel honored that others have suffered and sacrificed for us so that we might reap the benefit.

· **3:14, 15** The family of God includes all who have believed in him in the past, all who believe in the present, and all who will believe in the future. We are all a family because we have the same Father. He is the source of all creation, the rightful owner of everything. God promises his love and power to his family, the church (3:16-21). If we want to receive God's blessings, it is important that we stay in contact with other believers in the body of Christ. Those who isolate themselves from God's family and try to go it alone cut themselves off from God's power.

· **3:17-19** God's love is total, says Paul. It reaches every corner of our experience. It is *wide*—it covers the breadth of our own experience, and it reaches out to the whole world. God's love is *long*—it continues the length of our lives. It is *high*—it rises to the heights of our celebration and elation. His love is *deep*—it reaches to the depths of discouragement, despair, and even death. When you feel shut out or isolated, remember that you can never be lost

to God's love. For another prayer about God's immeasurable and inexhaustible love, see Paul's words in Romans 8:38, 39.

3:19 This "fullness" is expressed only in Christ (Colossians 2:9, 10). In union with Christ and through his empowering Spirit, we are complete. We have all the fullness of God available to us. But we must appropriate that fullness through faith and through prayer as we daily live for him. Paul's prayer for the Ephesians is also for you. You can ask the Holy Spirit to fill every aspect of your life to the fullest.

3:20, 21 This doxology—prayer of praise to God—ends part 1 of Ephesians. In the first section, Paul described the timeless role of the church. In part 2 (chapters 4–6), he will explain how church members should live in order to bring about the unity God wants. As in most of his books, Paul first lays a doctrinal foundation and then makes practical applications of the truths he has presented.

· **4:1, 2** God has chosen us to be Christ's representatives on earth. In light of this truth, Paul challenges us to live lives worthy of the calling we have received—the awesome privilege of being called Christ's very own. This includes being humble, gentle, patient, understanding, and peaceful. People are watching your life. Can they see Christ in you? How well are you doing as his representative?

· **4:1-6** "There is one body," says Paul. Unity does not just happen; we have to work at it. Often differences among people can lead to division, but this should not be true in the church. Instead of concentrating on what divides us, we should remember what unites us: *one* body, *one* Spirit, *one* future, *one* Lord, *one* faith, *one* baptism, *one* God! Have you learned to appreciate people who are different from you? Can you see how their differing gifts and viewpoints can help the church as it does God's work? Learn to enjoy the way we members of Christ's body complement one another. (See 1 Corinthians 12:12, 13 for more on this thought.)

4:2 No one is ever going to be perfect here on earth, so we must accept and love other Christians in spite of their faults. When we see faults in fellow believers, we should be patient and gentle. Is there someone whose actions or personality really annoys you? Rather than dwelling on that person's weaknesses or looking for

4:3
Col 3:14-15

4:4
Rom 12:5
1 Cor 12:12-13
Eph 2:16, 18

4:7
Rom 12:3
1 Cor 12:7

4:9
John 3:13
Acts 2:27
1 Pet 3:18

4:10
Eph 1:23

4:11
1 Cor 12:28

4:12
1 Cor 12:27

4:13
Eph 1:23
Col 1:28

other, making allowance for each other's faults because of your love. ³Make every effort to keep yourselves united in the Spirit, binding yourselves together with peace. ⁴For there is one body and one Spirit, just as you have been called to one glorious hope for the future. ⁵There is one Lord, one faith, one baptism, ⁶and one God and Father, who is over all and in all and living through all.

⁷However, he has given each one of us a special gift* through the generosity of Christ. ⁸That is why the Scriptures say,

"When he ascended to the heights,
   he led a crowd of captives
   and gave gifts to his people."*

⁹Notice that it says "he ascended." This clearly means that Christ also descended to our lowly world.* ¹⁰And the same one who descended is the one who ascended higher than all the heavens, so that he might fill the entire universe with himself.

¹¹Now these are the gifts Christ gave to the church: the apostles, the prophets, the evangelists, and the pastors and teachers. ¹²Their responsibility is to equip God's people to do his work and build up the church, the body of Christ. ¹³This will continue until we all come to such unity in our faith and knowledge of God's Son that we will be mature in the Lord, measuring up to the full and complete standard of Christ.

4:7 Greek *a grace.*   **4:8** Ps 68:18.   **4:9** Or *to the lowest parts of the earth.*

THE ONENESS OF ALL BELIEVERS

Believers are one in	Our unity is experienced in
Body	The fellowship of believers—the church
Spirit	The Holy Spirit, who activates the fellowship
Hope	That glorious future to which we are all called
Lord	Christ, to whom we all belong
Faith	Our singular commitment to Christ
Baptism	Baptism—the sign of entry into the church
God	God, who is our Father who keeps us for eternity

Too often believers are separated because of minor differences in doctrine. But Paul here shows those areas where Christians must agree to attain true unity. When believers have this unity of spirit, petty differences should never be allowed to dissolve that unity.

---

faults, pray for him or her. Then do even more—spend time together and see if you can learn to like him or her.

· **4:3** To build unity is one of the Holy Spirit's important roles. He leads, but we have to be willing to be led and to do our part to keep the peace. We do that by focusing on God, not on ourselves. For more about who the Holy Spirit is and what he does, see the notes on John 3:6; Acts 1:5; and Ephesians 1:13, 14.

· **4:4-7** All believers in Christ belong to one body; all are united under one head, Christ himself (see 1 Corinthians 12:12-27). Each believer has God-given abilities that can strengthen the whole body. Your special ability may seem small or large, but it is yours to use in God's service. Ask God to use your unique gifts to contribute to the strength and health of the body of believers.

4:6 God is "over all"—this shows his overruling care (transcendence). He is "in all" and "living through all"—this shows his active presence in the world and in the lives of believers (immanence). Any view of God that violates either his transcendence or his immanence does not paint a true picture of God.

4:8 In Psalm 68:18, God is pictured as a conqueror marching to the gates and taking tribute from the fallen city. Paul uses that picture to teach that Christ, in his crucifixion and resurrection, was victorious over Satan. When Christ ascended to heaven, he gave gifts to the church, some of which Paul discusses in 4:11-13.

4:9 The "lowly world" may be (1) the earth itself (lowly by comparison to heaven), (2) the grave, or (3) Hades (many believe Hades is the resting place of souls between death and resurrec-

tion). However we understand it, Christ is Lord of the whole universe, past, present, and future. Nothing or no one is hidden from him. The Lord of all came to earth and faced death to rescue all people. No one is beyond his reach.

· **4:11, 12** Our oneness in Christ does not destroy our individuality. The Holy Spirit has given each Christian special gifts for building up the church. Now that we have these gifts, it is crucial to use them. Are you spiritually mature, exercising the gifts God has given you? If you know what your gifts are, look for opportunities to serve. If you don't know, ask God to show you, perhaps with the help of your minister or Christian friends. Then, as you begin to recognize your special area of service, use your gifts to strengthen and encourage the church.

· **4:12, 13** God has given his church an enormous responsibility—to make disciples in every nation (Matthew 28:18-20). This involves preaching, teaching, healing, nurturing, giving, administering, building, and many other tasks. If we had to fulfill this command as individuals, we might as well give up without trying—it would be impossible. But God calls us as members of his body. Some of us can do one task; some can do another. Together we can obey God more fully than any of us could alone. It is a human tendency to overestimate what we can do by ourselves and to underestimate what we can do as a group. But as the body of Christ, we can accomplish more together than we would dream possible working by ourselves. Working together, the church can express the fullness of Christ (see the note on 3:19).

¹⁴Then we will no longer be immature like children. We won't be tossed and blown about by every wind of new teaching. We will not be influenced when people try to trick us with lies so clever they sound like the truth. ¹⁵Instead, we will speak the truth in love, growing in every way more and more like Christ, who is the head of his body, the church. ¹⁶He makes the whole body fit together perfectly. As each part does its own special work, it helps the other parts grow, so that the whole body is healthy and growing and full of love.

Living as Children of Light

¹⁷With the Lord's authority I say this: Live no longer as the Gentiles do, for they are hopelessly confused. ¹⁸Their minds are full of darkness; they wander far from the life God gives because they have closed their minds and hardened their hearts against him. ¹⁹They have no sense of shame. They live for lustful pleasure and eagerly practice every kind of impurity.

²⁰But that isn't what you learned about Christ. ²¹Since you have heard about Jesus and have learned the truth that comes from him, ²²throw off your old sinful nature and your former way of life, which is corrupted by lust and deception. ²³Instead, let the Spirit renew your thoughts and attitudes. ²⁴Put on your new nature, created to be like God—truly righteous and holy.

²⁵So stop telling lies. Let us tell our neighbors the truth, for we are all parts of the same body. ²⁶And "don't sin by letting anger control you."* Don't let the sun go down while you are still angry, ²⁷for anger gives a foothold to the devil.

²⁸If you are a thief, quit stealing. Instead, use your hands for good hard work, and then give generously to others in need. ²⁹Don't use foul or abusive language. Let everything you say be good and helpful, so that your words will be an encouragement to those who hear them.

4:26 Ps 4:4.

4:14 1 Cor 14:20 / Eph 6:11
4:15 Eph 1:22
4:16 Col 2:19
4:17 Rom 1:21 / Eph 2:2
4:19 Rom 1:24 / Col 3:5
4:22 Rom 6:6 / Col 3:5, 8-9 / Jas 1:21
4:23 Rom 12:2
4:24 2 Cor 5:17 / Col 3:10
4:25 †Zech 8:16 / Col 3:8-9
4:28 1 Thes 4:11
4:29 Matt 12:36 / Rom 14:19 / Col 3:8

· **4:14-16** Christ is the truth (John 14:6), and the Holy Spirit, who guides the church, is the Spirit of truth (John 16:13). Satan, by contrast, is the father of lies (John 8:44). As followers of Christ, we must be committed to the truth. This means both that our words should be honest and that our actions should reflect Christ's integrity. Speaking the truth in love is not always easy, convenient, or pleasant, but it is necessary if the church is going to do Christ's work in the world.

4:15 In describing the mature Christian, Paul says that one of the marks is the ability to "speak the truth in love." This sounds so simple, but it seems so hard for us to do. Some of us are fairly good at speaking the truth, but we forget to be loving. Some of us are good at being loving, but we don't have it in us to level with others if the truth is painful. The instruction here is to do both: Speak the truth, but do it in a loving manner. Think of the trouble we would spare ourselves if we followed this practice, especially in the church! When you have a problem with another believer, don't go to someone else with it. Go directly to that person, and speak the truth in love.

· **4:15, 16** Some Christians fear that any mistake will destroy their witness for the Lord. They see their own weaknesses, and they know that many non-Christians seem to have stronger character than they do. How can we grow more and more like Christ? The answer is that Christ forms us into a body—into a group of individuals who are united in their purpose and in their love for one another and for the Lord. If an individual stumbles, the rest of the group is there to pick that person up and help him or her walk with God again. If a person sins, he or she can find restoration through the church (Galatians 6:1) even as the rest of the body continues to witness to God's truth. As part of Christ's body, do you reflect part of Christ's character and carry out your special role in his work?

· **4:17** The natural tendency of human beings is to think their way away from God—leaving them "hopelessly confused." Intellectual pride, rationalizations, and excuses all keep people from God. Don't be surprised if people can't grasp the Good News. The Good News will seem foolish to those who forsake faith and rely on their own understanding.

· **4:17-24** People should be able to see a difference between Christians and non-Christians because of the way Christians live. We are to live full of light (5:8). Paul told the Ephesians to leave behind the old life of sin, since they were followers of Christ. Living the Christian life is a process. Although we have a new nature, we don't automatically think all good thoughts and express all right attitudes when we become new people in Christ. But if we keep listening to God, we will be changing all the time. As you look back over last year, do you see a process of change for the better in your thoughts, attitudes, and actions? Although change may be slow, it comes as you trust God to change you. For more about our new nature as believers, see Romans 6:6; 8:9; Galatians 5:16-26; Colossians 3:3-8.

4:22-24 Our old way of life before we believed in Christ is completely in the past. We should put it behind us like old clothes to be thrown away. When we decide to accept Christ's gift of salvation (2:8-10), it is both a one time decision, as well as a daily conscious commitment. We are not to be driven by desire and impulse. We must put on the new nature, head in the new direction, and have the new way of thinking that the Holy Spirit gives.

4:25 Lying to each other disrupts unity by creating conflicts and destroying trust. It tears down relationships and leads to open warfare in a church.

4:26, 27 The Bible doesn't tell us that we shouldn't feel angry, but it points out that it is important to handle our anger properly. If vented thoughtlessly, anger can hurt others and destroy relationships. If bottled up inside, it can cause us to become bitter and destroy us from within. Paul tells us to deal with our anger immediately in a way that builds relationships rather than destroys them. If we nurse our anger, we will give the devil an opportunity to divide us. Are you angry with someone right now? What can you do to resolve your differences? Don't let the day end before you begin to work on mending your relationship.

· **4:28-32** We can bring sorrow to the Holy Spirit by the way we live. Paul warns us against unwholesome language, bitterness, improper use of anger, harsh words, slander, and bad attitudes toward others. Instead of acting that way, we should be forgiving, just as God has forgiven us. Are you bringing sorrow or pleasing God with your attitudes and actions? Act in love toward your

4:30
Isa 63:10
Eph 1:13-14
1 Thes 5:19

4:31
Col 3:8
1 Pet 2:1

4:32
Col 3:12-13

5:1
Matt 5:48

5:2
John 13:34
Gal 1:14; 2:20

5:3
Col 3:5

5:4
Eph 4:29
Col 3:8

5:5
1 Cor 6:9-10
Col 3:5

5:6
Rom 1:18
Col 2:4, 8; 3:6

5:8
John 8:12
Eph 2:2

5:11
Rom 13:12

5:13
John 3:20-21

5:14
Isa 26:19; 51:17;
52:1; 60:1
John 5:25
Rom 13:11

5:16
Col 4:5

5:17
1 Thes 4:3

³⁰And do not bring sorrow to God's Holy Spirit by the way you live. Remember, he has identified you as his own,* guaranteeing that you will be saved on the day of redemption.

³¹Get rid of all bitterness, rage, anger, harsh words, and slander, as well as all types of evil behavior. ³²Instead, be kind to each other, tenderhearted, forgiving one another, just as God through Christ has forgiven you.

Living in the Light

5 Imitate God, therefore, in everything you do, because you are his dear children. ²Live a life filled with love, following the example of Christ. He loved us* and offered himself as a sacrifice for us, a pleasing aroma to God.

³Let there be no sexual immorality, impurity, or greed among you. Such sins have no place among God's people. ⁴Obscene stories, foolish talk, and coarse jokes—these are not for you. Instead, let there be thankfulness to God. ⁵You can be sure that no immoral, impure, or greedy person will inherit the Kingdom of Christ and of God. For a greedy person is an idolater, worshiping the things of this world.

⁶Don't be fooled by those who try to excuse these sins, for the anger of God will fall on all who disobey him. ⁷Don't participate in the things these people do. ⁸For once you were full of darkness, but now you have light from the Lord. So live as people of light! ⁹For this light within you produces only what is good and right and true.

¹⁰Carefully determine what pleases the Lord. ¹¹Take no part in the worthless deeds of evil and darkness; instead, expose them. ¹²It is shameful even to talk about the things that ungodly people do in secret. ¹³But their evil intentions will be exposed when the light shines on them, ¹⁴for the light makes everything visible. This is why it is said,

"Awake, O sleeper,
　　rise up from the dead,
　　and Christ will give you light."

Living by the Spirit's Power

¹⁵So be careful how you live. Don't live like fools, but like those who are wise. ¹⁶Make the most of every opportunity in these evil days. ¹⁷Don't act thoughtlessly, but understand what

4:30 Or *has put his seal on you.*　**5:2** Some manuscripts read *loved you.*

---

brothers and sisters in Christ, just as God acted in love by sending his Son to die for your sins.

4:30 The Holy Spirit within us is a guarantee that we belong to God. For more on this thought, see the note on 1:13, 14.

4:32 This is Christ's law of forgiveness as taught in the Gospels (Matthew 6:14, 15; 18:35; Mark 11:25). We also see it in the Lord's Prayer—"Forgive us our sins, as we forgive those who sin against us" (Luke 11:4). God forgives us, not because we forgive others, but solely because of his great mercy. As we come to understand his mercy, however, we will want to be like him. Having received forgiveness, we will pass it on to others. Those who are unwilling to forgive have not become one with Christ, who was willing to forgive even those who crucified him (Luke 23:34).

5:1, 2 Just as children imitate their parents, we should follow God's example. His great love for us led him to sacrifice himself so that we might live. Our love for others should be of the same kind—a love that goes beyond affection to self-sacrificing service.

· **5:4** Obscene stories and coarse jokes are so common that we begin to take them for granted. Paul cautions, however, that improper language should have no place in the Christian's conversation because it does not reflect God's gracious presence in us. How can we praise God and remind others of his goodness when we are speaking coarsely?

· **5:5-7** Paul does not forbid all contact with unbelievers. Jesus taught his followers to befriend sinners and lead them to him (Luke 5:30-32). Instead, Paul writes against the lifestyle of people who make excuses for bad behavior and recommend its practice to others—whether they are in the church or outside of it. Such people quickly pollute the church and endanger its

unity and purpose. We must befriend unbelievers if we are to lead them to Christ, but we must be wary of those who are viciously evil, immoral, or opposed to all that Christianity stands for. Such people are more likely to influence us for evil than we are to influence them for good.

· **5:8** As people who have light from the Lord, our actions should reflect our faith. We should live above reproach morally so that we will reflect God's goodness to others. Jesus stressed this truth in the Sermon on the Mount (Matthew 5:15, 16).

· **5:10-14** It is important to avoid the "worthless deeds of evil and darkness" (any pleasure or activity that results in sin), but we must go even further. Paul instructs us to expose these deeds, because our silence may be interpreted as approval. God needs people who will take a stand for what is right. Christians must lovingly speak out for what is true and right.

5:14 This is not a direct quote from Scripture but was probably taken from a hymn well known to the Ephesians. The hymn seems to have been based on Isaiah 26:19; 51:17; 52:1; 60:1; and Malachi 4:2. Paul was appealing to the Ephesians to wake up and realize the dangerous condition into which some of them had been slipping.

· **5:15, 16** By referring to these days as evil, Paul was communicating his sense of urgency because of evil's pervasiveness. We need the same sense of urgency because our days are also difficult. We must keep our standards high, act wisely, and do good whenever we can.

the Lord wants you to do. 18Don't be drunk with wine, because that will ruin your life. Instead, be filled with the Holy Spirit, 19singing psalms and hymns and spiritual songs among yourselves, and making music to the Lord in your hearts. 20And give thanks for everything to God the Father in the name of our Lord Jesus Christ.

5:18
Prov 20:1; 23:31
5:19
Col 3:16

Spirit-Guided Relationships: Wives and Husbands

21And further, submit to one another out of reverence for Christ.

22For wives, this means submit to your husbands as to the Lord. 23For a husband is the head of his wife as Christ is the head of the church. He is the Savior of his body, the church. 24As the church submits to Christ, so you wives should submit to your husbands in everything.

25For husbands, this means love your wives, just as Christ loved the church. He gave up his life for her 26to make her holy and clean, washed by the cleansing of God's word.* 27He did this to present her to himself as a glorious church without a spot or wrinkle or any other blemish. Instead, she will be holy and without fault. 28In the same way, husbands ought to love their wives as they love their own bodies. For a man who loves his wife actually shows love for himself. 29No one hates his own body but feeds and cares for it, just as Christ cares for the church. 30And we are members of his body.

5:21
1 Pet 5:5
5:22
Gen 3:16
5:23
1 Cor 11:3
5:26
John 15:3; 17:17
Heb 10:22
5:27
Eph 1:4
Col 1:22
5:29
1 Cor 12:27
5:30
1 Cor 6:15; 12:27

5:26 Greek *washed by water with the word.*

· **5:18** Paul contrasts getting drunk with wine, which produces a temporary "high," to being filled with the Spirit, which produces lasting joy. Getting drunk with wine is associated with the old way of life and its selfish desires. In Christ, we have a better joy, higher and longer lasting, to cure our depression, monotony, or tension. We should not be concerned with how much of the Holy Spirit we have but with how much of us the Holy Spirit has. Submit yourself daily to his leading and draw constantly on his power.

5:18, 19 The effects of alcohol are obvious, but what happens when we are under the influence of the Holy Spirit? In these verses, Paul lists three by-products of the Spirit's influence in our lives: singing, making music, and giving thanks. Paul did not intend to suggest that believers only discuss religious matters, but that whatever we do or say should be permeated with an attitude of joy, thankfulness to God, and encouragement of others. Instead of whining and complaining—which our culture has raised to an art form—we are to focus on the goodness of God and his mercies toward us. How would others characterize your words and attitudes?

5:20 When you feel down, you may find it difficult to give thanks. Take heart—in all things God works for our good if we love him and are called by him (Romans 8:28). Thank God, not for your problems but for the strength he is building in you through the difficult experiences of your life. You can be sure that God's perfect love will see you through.

· **5:21, 22** Submitting to another person is an often misunderstood concept. It does not mean becoming a doormat. Christ—at whose name "every knee should bow, in heaven and on earth and under the earth" (Philippians 2:10)—submitted his will to the Father, and we honor Christ by following his example. When we submit to God, we become more willing to obey his command to submit to others, that is, to subordinate our rights to theirs. In a marriage relationship, both husband and wife are called to submit. For the wife, this means willingly following her husband's leadership in Christ. For the husband, it means putting aside his own interests in order to care for his wife. Submission is rarely a problem in homes where both partners have a strong relationship with Christ and where each is concerned for the happiness of the other.

· **5:22-24** In Paul's day, women, children, and slaves were to submit to the head of the family: Slaves would submit until they were freed, male children until they grew up, and women and girls their whole lives. Paul emphasized the equality of all believers in Christ (Galatians 3:28), but he did not suggest overthrowing Roman society to achieve it. Instead, he counseled all believers to submit to one another by choice—wives to husbands and also husbands to wives; slaves to masters and also masters to slaves;

children to parents and also parents to children. This kind of mutual submission preserves order and harmony in the family, while it increases love and respect among family members.

· **5:22-24** Although some people have distorted Paul's teaching on submission by giving unlimited authority to husbands, we cannot get around it: Paul told wives to submit to their husbands. The fact that a teaching is not popular is no reason to discard it. One way to disarm the antagonism that the external culture may inject into the marriage relationship is to remember that the wife gets to submit and the husband gets to die. According to the Bible, the man is the spiritual head of the family, and his wife should acknowledge his leadership. But real spiritual leadership involves loving service (a form of dying). Just as Christ served the disciples, even to the point of washing their feet, so the husband is to serve his wife. A wise and Christ-honoring husband will not take advantage of his leadership role, and a wise and Christ-honoring wife will not try to undermine her husband's leadership. Either approach causes disunity and friction in marriage.

· **5:22-28** Why did Paul tell wives to submit and husbands to love? Perhaps Christian women, newly freed in Christ, found submission difficult; perhaps Christian men, used to the Roman custom of giving unlimited power to the head of the family, were not used to treating their wives with respect and love. Of course both husbands and wives should submit to each other (5:21), just as both should love each other.

· **5:25ff** Some Christians have thought that Paul was negative about marriage because of the counsel he gave in 1 Corinthians 7:32-38. These verses in Ephesians, however, show a high view of marriage. Here marriage is not a practical necessity or a cure for lust, but a picture of the relationship between Christ and his church! Why the apparent difference? Paul's counsel in 1 Corinthians was designed for a state of emergency during a time of persecution and crisis. Paul's counsel to the Ephesians is more the biblical ideal for marriage. Marriage, for Paul, is a holy union, a living symbol, a precious relationship that needs tender, self-sacrificing care.

· **5:25-30** Paul devotes twice as many words to telling husbands to love their wives as to telling wives to submit to their husbands. How should a man love his wife? (1) He should be willing to sacrifice everything for her, (2) make her well being of primary importance, and (3) care for her as he cares for his own body. No wife needs to fear submitting to a man who treats her in this way.

5:26, 27 Christ's death makes the church holy and clean. He cleanses us from the old ways of sin and sets us apart for his special sacred service (Hebrews 10:29; 13:12). Christ cleansed the church by the washing of baptism. Through baptism we are prepared for entrance into the church just as ancient Near Eastern

5:31
†Gen 2:24
Matt 19:5

5:33
1 Pet 3:1-2, 5

³¹As the Scriptures say, "A man leaves his father and mother and is joined to his wife, and the two are united into one."* ³²This is a great mystery, but it is an illustration of the way Christ and the church are one. ³³So again I say, each man must love his wife as he loves himself, and the wife must respect her husband.

Children and Parents

6:1
Col 3:20

6:2-3
†Exod 20:12
†Deut 5:16
Matt 15:4

6:4
Col 3:21

6 Children, obey your parents because you belong to the Lord,* for this is the right thing to do. ²"Honor your father and mother." This is the first commandment with a promise: ³If you honor your father and mother, "things will go well for you, and you will have a long life on the earth."*

⁴Fathers, do not provoke your children to anger by the way you treat them. Rather, bring them up with the discipline and instruction that comes from the Lord.

5:31 Gen 2:24.   **6:1** Or *Children, obey your parents who belong to the Lord;* some manuscripts read simply *Children, obey your parents.*   **6:2-3** Exod 20:12; Deut 5:16.

GOD'S ARMOR FOR US	Piece of Armor	Use	Application
We are engaged in a spiritual battle—all believers find themselves subject to the devil's attacks because they are no longer on the devil's side. Thus, Paul tells us to use *every piece* of God's armor to resist the devil's attacks and to stand true to God in the midst of those attacks.	Belt	Truth	The devil fights with lies, and sometimes his lies *sound* like truth; but only believers have God's truth, which can defeat the devil's lies.
	Body armor	Righteousness	The devil often attacks our heart—the seat of our emotions, self-worth, and trust. God's righteousness is the body armor that protects our heart and ensures his approval. He approves of us because he loves us and sent his Son to die for us.
	Shoes	Peace that comes from the Good News	The devil wants us to think that telling others the Good News is a worthless and hopeless task—the size of the task is too big and the negative responses are too much to handle. But the shoes God gives us are the motivation to continue to proclaim the true peace that is available in God—news everyone needs to hear.
	Shield	Faith	What *we* see are the devil's attacks in the form of insults, setbacks, and temptations. But the shield of faith protects us from the devil's fiery arrows. With God's perspective, we can see beyond our circumstances and know that ultimate victory is ours.
	Helmet	Salvation	The devil wants to make us doubt God, Jesus, and our salvation. The helmet protects our mind from doubting God's saving work for us.
	Sword	Word of God	The sword is the only weapon of *offense* in this list of armor. There are times when we need to take the offensive against the devil. When we are tempted, we need to trust in the truth of God's Word.

---

brides were prepared for marriage by a ceremonial bath. It is God's Word that cleanses us (John 17:17; Titus 3:5).

5:31-33 The union of husband and wife merges two persons in such a way that little can affect one without also affecting the other. Oneness in marriage does not mean losing your personality in the personality of the other. Instead, it means caring for your spouse as you care for yourself, learning to anticipate his or her needs, helping the other person become all he or she can be. The creation story tells of God's plan that husband and wife should be one (Genesis 2:24), and Jesus also referred to this plan (Matthew 19:4-6).

· **6:1, 2** There is a difference between obeying and honoring. To obey means to do as one is told; to honor means to respect and love. Children are not commanded to disobey God in obeying their parents. Adult children are not asked to be subservient to domineering parents. Children are to obey while under their parents' care, but the responsibility to honor parents is for life.

· **6:1-4** If our faith in Christ is real, it will usually prove itself in our relationships at home with those who know us best. Children and parents have a responsibility to each other. Children should

honor their parents even if the parents are demanding and unfair. Parents should care gently for their children, even if the children are disobedient and unpleasant. Ideally, of course, Christian parents and Christian children will relate to each other with thoughtfulness and love. This will happen if both parents and children put the others' interests above their own—that is, if they submit to one another.

6:3 Some societies honor their elders. They respect their wisdom, defer to their authority, and pay attention to their comfort and happiness. This is how Christians should act. Where elders are respected, long life is a blessing, not a burden to them.

6:4 The purpose of parental discipline is to help children grow, not to exasperate and provoke them to anger or discouragement (see also Colossians 3:21). Parenting is not easy—it takes lots of patience to raise children in a loving, Christ-honoring manner. But frustration and anger should not be causes for discipline. Instead, parents should act in love, treating their children as Jesus treats the people he loves. This is vital to children's development and to their understanding of what Christ is like.

Slaves and Masters

5Slaves, obey your earthly masters with deep respect and fear. Serve them sincerely as you would serve Christ. 6Try to please them all the time, not just when they are watching you. As slaves of Christ, do the will of God with all your heart. 7Work with enthusiasm, as though you were working for the Lord rather than for people. 8Remember that the Lord will reward each one of us for the good we do, whether we are slaves or free.

9Masters, treat your slaves in the same way. Don't threaten them; remember, you both have the same Master in heaven, and he has no favorites.

6:5-7
//Col 3:22-23
Titus 2:9-10

6:8
Col 3:24-25

6:9
Job 31:13-14
Col 4:1

The Whole Armor of God

10A final word: Be strong in the Lord and in his mighty power. 11Put on all of God's armor so that you will be able to stand firm against all strategies of the devil. 12For we* are not fighting against flesh-and-blood enemies, but against evil rulers and authorities of the unseen world, against mighty powers in this dark world, and against evil spirits in the heavenly places.

13Therefore, put on every piece of God's armor so you will be able to resist the enemy in the time of evil. Then after the battle you will still be standing firm. 14Stand your ground, putting on the belt of truth and the body armor of God's righteousness. 15For shoes, put on the peace that comes from the Good News so that you will be fully prepared.* 16In addition to all of these, hold up the shield of faith to stop the fiery arrows of the devil.* 17Put on salvation as your helmet, and take the sword of the Spirit, which is the word of God.

18Pray in the Spirit at all times and on every occasion. Stay alert and be persistent in your prayers for all believers everywhere.*

19And pray for me, too. Ask God to give me the right words so I can boldly explain God's mysterious plan that the Good News is for Jews and Gentiles alike.* 20I am in chains now, still preaching this message as God's ambassador. So pray that I will keep on speaking boldly for him, as I should.

6:11
Rom 13:12
1 Thes 5:8

6:12
Eph 3:10

6:14
Isa 11:5; 59:17
1 Thes 5:8

6:15
Isa 52:7

6:16
1 Jn 5:4

6:17
Isa 59:17
1 Thes 5:8
Heb 4:12

6:18
Rom 8:26-27
Phil 4:6
Col 4:2-3

6:19
Col 4:3-4

6:12 Some manuscripts read *you*.   **6:15** Or *For shoes, put on the readiness to preach the Good News of peace with God*.   **6:16** Greek *the evil one*.   **6:18** Greek *all of God's holy people*.   **6:19** Greek *explain the mystery of the Good News;* some manuscripts read simply *explain the mystery*.

· **6:5** Slaves played a significant part in this society. There were several million of them in the Roman Empire at this time. Because many slaves and owners had become Christians, the early church had to deal straightforwardly with the question of master/slave relations. Paul's statement neither condemns nor condones slavery. Instead, it tells masters and slaves how to live together in Christian households. In Paul's day, women, children, and slaves had few rights. In the church, however, they had freedoms that society denied them. Paul tells husbands, parents, and masters to be caring.

· **6:6-8** Paul's instructions encourage responsibility and integrity on the job. Christian employees should do their jobs as if Jesus Christ were their supervisor. And Christian employers should treat their employees fairly and with respect. Can you be trusted to do your best, even when the boss is not around? Do you work hard and with enthusiasm? Do you treat your employees as people, not machines? Remember that no matter whom you work for, and no matter who works for you, the one you ultimately should want to please is your Father in heaven.

6:9 Although Christians may be at different levels in earthly society, we are all equal before God. He does not play favorites; no one is more important than anyone else. Paul's letter to Philemon stresses the same point: Philemon, the master, and Onesimus, his slave, were brothers in Christ.

· **6:10-17** In the Christian life we battle against rulers and authorities (the powerful evil forces of fallen angels headed by the devil, who is a vicious fighter, see 1 Peter 5:8). To withstand their attacks, we must depend on God's strength and use every piece of his armor. Paul is not only giving this counsel to the church, the body of Christ, but to all individuals within the church. The whole body needs to be armed. As you do battle against the "mighty

powers in this dark world," fight in the strength of the church, whose power comes from the Holy Spirit.

· **6:12** These who are not "flesh-and-blood enemies" are demons over whom the devil has control. They are not mere fantasies—they are very real. We face a powerful army whose goal is to defeat Christ's church. When we believe in Christ, these beings become our enemies, and they try every device to turn us away from him and back to sin. Although we are assured of victory, we must engage in the struggle until Christ returns, because Satan is constantly battling against all who are on the Lord's side. We need supernatural power to defeat Satan, and God has provided this by giving us his Holy Spirit within us and his armor surrounding us. If you feel discouraged, remember Jesus' words to Peter: "Upon this rock I will build my church, and all the powers of hell will not conquer it" (Matthew 16:18).

· **6:18** How can anyone pray at all times? One way is to make quick, brief prayers your habitual response to every situation you meet throughout the day. Another way is to order your life around God's desires and teachings so that your very life becomes a prayer. You don't have to isolate yourself from other people and from daily work in order to pray constantly. You can make prayer your life and your life a prayer while living in a world that needs God's powerful influence. We also should pray for all believers in Christ; so pray for the Christians you know and for the church around the world.

· **6:19, 20** Undiscouraged and undefeated, Paul wrote powerful letters of encouragement from prison. Paul did not ask the Ephesians to pray that his chains would be removed but that he would continue to speak fearlessly for Christ in spite of them. God can use us in any circumstance to do his will. Even as we pray for a change in our circumstances, we should also pray that God will accomplish his plan through us right where we are. Knowing God's eternal purpose for us will help us through the difficult times.

6:21
Acts 20:4
2 Tim 4:12
Titus 3:12

6:22
Col 4:7-9

6:23
Gal 6:16
2 Thes 3:16

Final Greetings

21 To bring you up to date, Tychicus will give you a full report about what I am doing and how I am getting along. He is a beloved brother and faithful helper in the Lord's work. 22 I have sent him to you for this very purpose—to let you know how we are doing and to encourage you.

23 Peace be with you, dear brothers and sisters,* and may God the Father and the Lord Jesus Christ give you love with faithfulness. 24 May God's grace be eternally upon all who love our Lord Jesus Christ.

6:23 Greek *brothers.*

6:21 Tychicus is also mentioned in Acts 20:4, Colossians 4:7, 2 Timothy 4:12, and Titus 3:12.

· **6:24** This letter was written to the church at Ephesus, but it was also meant for circulation among other churches. In this letter, Paul highlights the supremacy of Christ, gives information on both the nature of the church and on how church members should live, and stresses the unity of all believers—male, female, parent, child, master, slave—regardless of sex, nationality, or social rank. The home and the church are difficult places to live the Christian life, because our real self comes through to those who know us well. Close relationships between imperfect people can lead to trouble—or to increased faith and deepened dependence on God. We can build unity in our churches through willing submission to Christ's leadership and humble service to one another.

STUDY QUESTIONS

Thirteen lessons for individual or group study

HOW TO USE THIS BIBLE STUDY

It's always exciting to get more than you expect. And that's what you'll find in this Bible study guide—much more than you expect. Our goal was to write thoughtful, practical, dependable, and application-oriented studies of God's word.

This study guide contains the complete text of the selected Bible book. The commentary is accurate, complete, and loaded with unique charts, maps, and profiles of Bible people.

With the Bible text, extensive notes and helps, and questions to guide discussion, these Life Application Bible Studies have everything you need in one place.

The lessons in this Bible study guide will work for large classes as well as small-group studies. To get everyone involved in your discussions, encourage participants to answer the questions before each meeting.

Each lesson is divided into five easy-to-lead sections. The section called "Reflect" introduces you and the members of your group to a specific area of life touched by the lesson. "Read" shows which chapters to read and which notes and other features to use. Additional questions help you understand the passage. "Realize" brings into focus the biblical principle to be learned with questions, a special insight, or both. "Respond" helps you make connections with your own situation and personal needs. The questions are designed to help you find areas in your life where you can apply the biblical truths. "Resolve" helps you map out action plans for that day.

Begin and end each lesson with prayer, asking for the Holy Spirit's guidance, direction, and wisdom.

Recommended time allotments for each section of a lesson are as follows:

Segment	60 minutes	90 miutes
Reflect on your life	*5 minutes*	*10 minutes*
Read the passage	*10 minutes*	*15 minutes*
Realize the principle	*15 minutes*	*20 minutes*
Respond to the message	*20 minutes*	*30 minutes*
Resolve to take action	*10 minutes*	*15 minutes*

All five sections work together to help a person learn the lessons, live out the principles, and obey the commands taught in the Bible.

Also, at the end of each lesson, there is a section entitled "More for studying other themes in this section." These questions will help you lead the group in studying other parts of each section not covered in depth by the main lesson.

But don't just listen to God's word. You must do what it says. Otherwise, you are only fooling yourselves. For if you listen to the word and don't obey, it is like glancing at your face in a mirror. You see yourself, walk away, and forget what you look like. But if you look carefully into the perfect law that sets you free, and if you do what it says and don't forget what you heard, then God will bless you for doing it (James 1:22-25).

LESSON 1
RUNNING FROM FREEDOM
GALATIANS 1:1-10

REFLECT
on your life

1 Finish this sentence: "Freedom is _____

_____

_____

_____

2 People talk a lot about freedom, but when can freedom be frightening?

_____

_____

_____

READ
the passage

Read the two-page introduction to Galatians, the chart "The Marks of the True Gospel and of False Gospels," Galatians 1:1-10, and the following notes:

❒ 1:1   ❒ 1:2   ❒ 1:3-5   ❒ 1:6   ❒ 1:7   ❒ 1:10

3 Who were the Galatians? Who were the Judaizers?

_____

_____

_____

4 For what reasons did Paul write this book? What is the central message of Galatians?

_____

_____

_____

_____

5 What was the problem that Paul was confronting? Why did he react so harshly to this particular problem?

_____

_____

_____

_____

6 In what ways were the Judaizers also guilty of distorting the nature and purpose of the law?

_____

_____

_____

7 According to the opening verses, what are the essential elements of the gospel?

_____

_____

_____

8 What might have motivated the Judaizers to teach what they did?

_____

_____

_____

REALIZE
the principle

9 What danger is there in trying to combine the law and the gospel in this way?

_____

_____

_____

_____

10 Why would the Galatian believers, many of whom were Gentiles, be willing to live by the restrictions of the law when their salvation had come solely by grace?

_____

_____

_____

_____

The gospel gives us freedom on two levels: (1) We are free from sin's hold on us and its eternal consequences in our lives; and (2) we are free to serve God and others out of gratitude for God's grace. But sometimes our freedom makes us feel uncomfortable. Freedom can be frightening if it seems that we no longer have firm boundaries for our actions. And freedom to serve is of little comfort if we don't feel confident that we are doing what God wants. In the face of such uncertainties, we may be tempted to trade away our Christ-bought freedom for a set of rules and regulations. We should be on guard against those who would have us live according to a checklist of dos and don'ts.

11 Why is it so difficult for us to remember that we have freedom in Christ?

_____

_____

_____

_____

RESPOND
to the message

12 What rules do Christians today try to add to the gospel? What is dangerous about these rules?

_____

_____

_____

_____

13 How might these rules pervert the true message of the gospel?

_____

_____

_____

14 Look at the chart "The Marks of the True Gospel and of False Gospels." In what ways does your church exemplify the marks of the true gospel?

_____

_____

_____

_____

15 If new believers or non-Christians visited your church, what rules would they think a person has to obey in order to be a good Christian?

_____

_____

_____

_____

16 If non-Christians heard *you* talk about the Christian life, what rules might they conclude that you have to keep to be a Christian?

_____

_____

_____

_____

17 In what ways do you tend to run away from freedom in Christ?

_____

_____

_____

_____

_____

RESOLVE
to take action

18 Think of some ways that you could use your freedom in Christ to serve God and others. What could you do this week?

_____

_____

_____

A How does Satan do his destructive work among God's people? How can you identify a work of Satan?

MORE
for studying
other themes
in this section

B Paul's critics charged that he was diluting the gospel in order to make it more attractive to unbelievers. How can we avoid this danger without sliding into legalism?

C Paul accused the Judaizers of trying to win the approval of men. How do we sometimes act to secure the approval of others rather than God? Why is it difficult for us to seek God's approval above the approval of others?

LESSON 2
CONSTRUCTIVE CONFRONTATION
GALATIANS 1:11–2:21

R
REFLECT
on your life

1 How do you react when you see someone you love or respect doing something that you know is wrong? What should you do?

_____

_____

_____

_____

_____

R
READ
the passage

Read Galatians 1:11–2:21, the chart "Judaizers versus Paul," and the following notes:

❐ 1:11ff   ❐ 1:15, 16   ❐ 1:15-24   ❐ 2:2   ❐ 2:2, 3   ❐ 2:6   ❐ 2:11   ❐ 2:11ff

2 Who were the Judaizers, and what was their complaint against Paul? Why did their point of view make sense to them?

_____

_____

_____

_____

3 Why was the conflict over keeping the Jewish law such a big issue for the early church?

_____

_____

_____

_____

4 Why were Paul's credentials and the approval of the Jerusalem elders important in his battle against the Judaizers?

_____

_____

_____

_____

5 Why did Paul think it was necessary to confront the Judaizers so forcefully?

_____

_____

_____

_____

REALIZE
the principle

6 Why did Paul have to oppose Peter publicly? How would you have advised him to handle the situation?

_____

_____

_____

_____

7 What methods, attitudes, or principles do you see in these verses that would help in dealing constructively with dissent in the church today?

_____

_____

_____

_____

Confrontation can often be awkward and harmful, but Paul was able to confront constructively. We can learn some important lessons about how to handle this difficult aspect of human relationships by looking at Paul's approach. First, Paul was concerned that others saw him as a person of integrity—a credible witness. Second, he was well prepared—knowledgeable, articulate, and focused. Third, he had a constructive purpose—to build others up, not to tear people down or build himself up. Fourth, he was constantly seeking God's perspective—divine truth must prevail over self-interest or personal position. When faced with the need to confront others about their words or actions, we should follow Paul's example of constructive confrontation.

8 What makes it difficult for Christians to honestly and lovingly confront others in their churches?

_____

_____

_____

_____

RESPOND
to the message

9 What would make it difficult for you to talk to others about their wrong behavior or attitudes?

_____

_____

_____

10 What credentials do you have that undergird your authority to confront others on important matters of Christian belief or practice?

_____

_____

_____

11 How do you prepare when you are going to talk to someone about a touchy situation? What could you do to be better prepared?

_____

_____

_____

12 What can you do to make sure that your purpose is to build up and not tear down? What difference will this make in how you approach someone?

_____

_____

_____

13 How would you handle a situation where both sides think that they are in God's will?

_____

_____

_____

14 What can you do right now to improve the way you confront others?

_____

_____

_____

_____

15 What can you do to improve the way you respond to others who confront you?

_____

_____

_____

16 Whom do you need to confront about their words or actions? Pray that God will give you wisdom to know whether or not action should be taken. How should you approach the situation?

_____

_____

_____

_____

RESOLVE
to take action

A What was in Paul's past that further strengthened his case against the Judaizers? What aspects of your past lend credibility to your witness?

B Why do you think the Jerusalem elders reminded Paul to consider the needs of the poor? Why do we still need reminders to care for the poor?

C What does it mean to be "crucified with Christ"? What does it mean to have "died to the law"?

D Review the chart "Do We Still Have to Obey the Old Testament Laws?" What are the helpful purposes of the three aspects of the law? Where might a person go wrong in applying these guidelines? How is the law helpful in your life?

MORE
for studying
other themes
in this section

LESSON 3
PRISONERS AND OUTLAWS
GALATIANS 3:1-23

REFLECT
on your life

1 Describe an event in your life that shook your sense of security. What did it take to feel safe again?

_____

_____

_____

_____

_____

READ
the passage

Read Galatians 3:1-23, the chart "Three Distortions of Christianity," and the following notes:

❏ 3:2, 3   ❏ 3:5   ❏ 3:10   ❏ 3:11   ❏ 3:18, 19   ❏ 3:19, 20   ❏ 3:21, 22

2 How does the example of Abraham show the superiority of faith over observing the law (3:6-9, 15-18)?

_____

_____

_____

_____

3 What does the sentence "It is through faith that a righteous person has life" mean (3:11)? How would you answer someone who complained that this bases the Christian life too much on personal experience?

_____

_____

_____

_____

_____

4 For Christians, what is the purpose of the law (3:21-23)?

_____

_____

_____

_____

_____

5 How does each of the three distortions of Christianity (see the chart) diminish the gospel? How can each one lead believers astray?

REALIZE
the principle

_____

_____

_____

_____

_____

_____

_____

Christ has set us free, but as we attempt to live by faith, we are still in danger of falling into certain traps. Wanting the security of being able to earn our salvation, we add human traditions, standards, and rules to our faith. We slip back into performing a certain way, serving or doing good deeds as if we needed to impress God or earn his approval. And wanting to feel good, we let ourselves be directed by our ever-changing emotions. The security trap makes us prisoners just as surely as if the law held us in its grip. The emotional trap can result in our becoming "outlaws," deciding for ourselves what is right and wrong. Either way, we rob ourselves of the true joy and security we share with all who have accepted God's promise of salvation by faith alone.

6 What rules and regulations have Christians added to the gospel? What problems has this caused?

RESPOND
to the message

_____

_____

_____

_____

_____

7 In what ways have Christians blended too much personal experience into the gospel? What problems has this caused?

_____

_____

_____

_____

_____

_____

_____

8 How can Christians avoid falling into the security trap?

_____

_____

_____

_____

_____

9 How can Christians avoid falling into the emotional trap?

_____

_____

_____

_____

_____

RESOLVE
to take action

10 Which of the three distortions mentioned in the chart has given you the most trouble in your faith? How can you avoid both legalistic and lawless Christianity?

_____

_____

_____

_____

_____

11 What can you do to restore balance in your Christian life? What first steps can you take this week?

_____

_____

_____

_____

_____

_____

A What blessing did God promise to Abraham? How do we receive this by faith?

B What place do today's Jews have in God's plan of salvation? How should we, as Christians, relate to them?

MORE
for studying
other themes
in this section

LESSON 4
LOVE, LOVE, LOVE
GALATIANS 3:24–4:31

R
REFLECT
on your life

1 Who are the most difficult people to love? Why?

_____

_____

_____

_____

_____

R
READ
the passage

Read Galatians 3:24–4:31 and the following notes:

❒ 3:24, 25   ❒ 3:28   ❒ 4:3-7   ❒ 4:5-7   ❒ 4:15   ❒ 4:17   ❒ 4:19

2 What does it mean to be "true children of Abraham" (3:29)?

_____

_____

_____

_____

_____

3 What important qualities of spiritual fatherhood and brotherhood does Paul show us in this passage (4:8-20)?

_____

_____

_____

_____

4 In spite of Paul's often harsh words, what evidence do you see in this passage of his genuine love for the Galatian believers?

_____

_____

_____

_____

_____

_____

5 What benefits and responsibilities do believers have as God's children that they didn't have before coming to know him?

_____

_____

_____

_____

_____

_____

REALIZE
the principle

Paul had every right to be angry with the Galatian Christians. They had turned away from the truth that he had worked so hard to teach them and had returned to the empty religion that had formerly enslaved them and robbed them of so much joy. But Paul cared enough about them to grieve over their condition. He was their brother because he too was one of God's adopted sons, and he was their father because he had led many of them to Christ. Paul's great love made it impossible for him to turn his back on them or to act selfishly to further his own ends. That kind of love could come only from God. And because God loves us, we should keep loving others even when they let us down.

6 In what ways might other Christians disappoint us?

_____

_____

_____

_____

_____

_____

R
RESPOND
to the message

7 Why is it difficult to find unconditional love practiced in the church? How might we encourage believers to care unselfishly for each other?

_____

_____

_____

_____

_____

_____

8 How might telling the truth to people create enemies for oneself? How might telling the truth cause people to turn against their other friends?

_____

_____

_____

_____

_____

_____

9 How can you tell whether someone truly wants what is best for you and is not acting out of selfish motives?

_____

_____

_____

_____

_____

_____

10 What excuses do we often give for withdrawing our love from others when they backslide in their Christian lives?

_____

_____

_____

_____

_____

_____

11 Who has cared enough for you to keep loving you through a difficult time? Find an opportunity soon to thank that person for his or her unselfish love.

_____

_____

_____

_____

12 Who do you feel is letting you down right now? How can you remember to keep on loving and caring for that person?

_____

_____

_____

_____

A What does it mean to be "united with Christ in baptism" (3:27)? What does it mean to "put on Christ" (3:27)?

B What does it mean that Christ came at "the right time"? Why is it so difficult for us to wait for God's timing?

C How does the story of Abraham's two sons add to Paul's earlier arguments regarding the nature of the law and of God's grace? Why might this be especially meaningful to the Galatians? What does it mean to you?

D What were the certain days and months that were being observed? How does this relate to special days and seasons, such as Lent, in the Christian church?

E Paul said that he was in labor pains until "Christ is fully developed in your lives" (4:19). What does this mean for us? When is the process complete?

LESSON 5
WHAT FREEDOM BRINGS
GALATIANS 5:1-26

REFLECT
on your life

1 If a call-in radio program asked listeners to explain what *virtue* means, how would callers answer?

_____

_____

_____

_____

READ
the passage

Read Galatians 5:1-26, the two charts "Vices and Virtues" and "Our Wrong Desires versus the Fruit of the Spirit," and the following notes:

❐ 5:6   ❐ 5:13   ❐ 5:16-18   ❐ 5:17   ❐ 5:19-21   ❐ 5:22, 23   ❐ 5:23

❐ 5:24   ❐ 5:25

2 What does it mean to fall away from God's grace (5:4)? What keeps us from living by grace?

_____

_____

_____

_____

3 How does faith express itself through love (5:6)? What makes this a struggle for most believers?

_____

_____

_____

_____

4 How do the vices that Paul mentions (5:19-21) undermine relationships with both God and people? Which vices do you consider to be the most dangerous for your church?

_____

_____

_____

_____

_____

5 Which is more important: eliminating vice or cultivating virtue? Why?

_____

_____

_____

REALIZE
the principle

Living the Christian life is a two-sided battle. On the one hand, we fight to remove vices from our life and avoid temptation. But a complete victory on this side alone is not enough. We also need to fill our life with virtues or expressions of our spiritual gifts. But we may not know how to cultivate these virtues, and we may even wonder what they are. Paul gives us a clear picture with the list commonly called _the fruit of the Spirit_. To have this fruit, we must reject our sinful desires and ask the Spirit to mold us into the kind of people Jesus has freed us to be. Then others will begin to see in us the delightful fruit of our Christ-bought freedom.

6 What does it mean to crucify the sinful nature (5:24)? If our sinful nature has been crucified, why are we still tempted to sin?

_____

_____

_____

_____

7 What does your church teach new Christians about how to grow in the fruit of the Spirit? Why is there often confusion about this important area of Christian growth?

_____

_____

_____

_____

R
RESPOND
to the message

8 Why does it seem so much easier for vice to manifest itself in our lives rather than virtue?

_____

_____

_____

_____

_____

9 In what way is the fruit of the Spirit the result of God's grace? In what way is it the result of our obedience?

_____

_____

_____

_____

10 Which of the virtues listed is the most developed in your life? Where have you seen the most progress over the last year? Rate your progress on each:

	No progress	*Some progress*	*Great progress*
Love	_____	_____	_____
Joy	_____	_____	_____
Peace	_____	_____	_____
Patience	_____	_____	_____
Kindness	_____	_____	_____
Goodness	_____	_____	_____
Faithfulness	_____	_____	_____
Gentleness	_____	_____	_____
Self-control	_____	_____	_____

R
RESOLVE
to take action

11 Which fruit of the Spirit has God been helping you develop recently in your life? Which is the least developed in your life or in most need of attention?

_____

_____

_____

_____

12 Which fruit of the Spirit do you most want to develop further? Where in your life is this most needed: home, school, work, church, or in the community?

_____

_____

_____

_____

13 Ask God to make you more and more like Christ in this area. What specific steps can you take to bring your behavior in line with the Holy Spirit's leading?

_____

_____

_____

_____

_____

MORE
for studying
other themes
in this section

A What does it mean to use Christian freedom responsibly? How will this appear to others? Give an example of one way that you are limiting your freedom for the sake of others.

B How did insistence on circumcision devalue what Christ had done on the cross? What works do some Christians insist on performing today?

C In what ways are modern-day believers still being persecuted for the sake of righteousness? How are you persecuted? How does God want you to respond to persecution?

D In this chapter, Paul is speaking strongly and directly. He does not pull any punches, yet his words are instructive for the Galatians. What is the difference between constructive confrontation and destructive criticism?

E How can you know when you are living "by the Spirit" (5:25)? What can you do to get back in step with him?

LESSON 6
SETTING OTHERS FREE
GALATIANS 6:1-18

REFLECT
on your life

1 In what general ways can we help others?

_____

_____

_____

2 What kinds of personal problems do people have?

_____

_____

_____

_____

READ
the passage

Read Galatians 6:1-18 and the following notes:

❑ 6:1-3   ❑ 6:4   ❑ 6:6   ❑ 6:7, 8   ❑ 6:14   ❑ 6:15   ❑ 6:18

3 What does it mean to help someone "back onto the right path" (6:1)?

_____

_____

_____

4 What is the "law of Christ" (6:2), and how can a person fulfill it?

_____

_____

_____

_____

_____

5 In what ways do we reap what we sow (6:7)?

_____

_____

_____

_____

_____

_____

6 We are told to share each other's troubles and problems while being responsible for our own conduct. How is it possible to do both?

_____

_____

_____

_____

_____

_____

There are many reasons for growing weary in doing good. Lack of appreciation,
relapses in those we've helped, and the pressures of coping with our own problems all wear us down. Also, our confidence may be undermined by a sense of
personal inadequacy. And there are many distractions, including selfishness,
critical attitude promoters, and unnecessary side issues. All of these factors
cause us to focus on ourselves. It's hard to help others with their troubles when
we aren't sure we can handle our own. But strength comes when we reach out to
others. In serving others, we not only obey the law of Christ but also experience
a refreshing freedom from our own self-centeredness.

7 Why is it especially important to do good to those within the church?

_____

_____

_____

_____

_____

_____

8 What should be our attitude toward other believers' failures?

_____

_____

_____

_____

_____

_____

9 What is the believer's responsibility for carrying his or her own "load"?

_____

_____

_____

_____

_____

10 What is the believer's responsibility in sharing others' troubles?

_____

_____

_____

11 What gets in the way of helping others with their troubles?

_____

_____

_____

_____

12 How can we overcome these interfering factors and make our churches more caring?

_____

_____

_____

_____

_____

_____

13 Whom do you know who is struggling and could use your support? Think of some practical ways in which you could help that person. What steps could you begin to take this week?

_____

_____

_____

_____

_____

RESOLVE
to take action

A What is the "right time" to which Paul refers (6:9)? And what is the "harvest" he promises? How is that relevant?

B In what ways were the Judaizers boasting in the flesh of their followers? What is wrong with being proud of the impact you have had on others? How do some Christians fall into the trap of boasting?

C What "scars" of Jesus did Paul bear (6:17)? Why were his scars significant to those who knew him? What scars of Jesus do you bear?

D Why is it so important to be supportive of our teachers? Why is it important to care for the financial needs of our pastors?

MORE
for studying
other themes
in this section

LESSON 7
ALL IN THE FAMILY
EPHESIANS 1:1-14

R REFLECT
on your life

1 Describe one or two of your happiest moments growing up in your family.

_____

_____

_____

_____

_____

2 What are some of the benefits of being part of a happy family?

_____

_____

_____

_____

_____

R READ
the passage

Read the two-page introduction to Ephesians, the chart "Our True Identity in Christ," Ephesians 1:1-14, and the following notes:

❐ 1:1   ❐ 1:3   ❐ 1:4   ❐ 1:7, 8   ❐ 1:11   ❐ 1:13, 14

3 What does it mean to be adopted as God's children (1:5)?

_____

_____

_____

_____

4 What does it mean to be "under the authority of Christ" (1:10)?

_____

_____

_____

_____

_____

5 What does being under the authority of Christ imply about learning to work together? What does this suggest about exclusiveness in the body of Christ?

_____

_____

_____

_____

6 How does Christ identify all believers (1:13)?

_____

_____

_____

_____

7 From the chart "Our True Identity in Christ," what conclusions can we draw about the nature of the church? about our relationships with other believers?

REALIZE
the principle

_____

_____

_____

_____

_____

Families are important because in them we discover who we are. A strong, supportive family helps to build our confidence and sense of worth. Our Christian identity is bolstered by our involvement in God's family. Paul understood the importance of the church as a kind of family that teaches us what it means to be a Christian. All believers share a common identity based on faith in Christ. And our common identity is so much more important than our differences. All Christians should remember that they live together in God's family with a common heritage, a common identity, a common purpose, and a common eternal future; and they should seek to live in harmony.

8 What does Ephesians 1:1-14 teach about what Christians have in common?

_____

_____

_____

_____

RESPOND
to the message

9 What characteristics of healthy family relationships should be evident in our dealings with others in the church?

_____

_____

_____

_____

10 What tends to weaken the sense of family in your church? What can be done to guard against those conditions?

_____

_____

_____

_____

11 What can be done to strengthen the sense of family in your church?

_____

_____

_____

_____

RESOLVE
to take action

12 Thank God for choosing you to be a part of his family. Ask him to show you what else you can do to be a positive contributor to the family. What can you do this week to be a better member of your church family?

_____

_____

_____

A What does the title "apostle" mean? What special qualification does Paul have for using this title? What credentials are important in churches today? Why?

B Why was Ephesus such a strategically important church for the spread of the gospel? What is strategic about your church's location?

C Predestination is viewed differently by various denominations. Regardless of the differences in interpretation, what are the positive implications of being "chosen"?

D What is the "mysterious plan" (1:9) to which Paul refers, and how will it be revealed when the time is fulfilled? What part of the secret plan has been revealed? What remains a mystery for us?

E What are some of the terms Paul uses to emphasize our standing as God's chosen children? What rights and privileges does this give us?

F God works out everything "according to his plan" (1:11). Describe God's purpose and plan for your life.

MORE
for studying
other themes
in this section

LESSON 8
ALIVE!
EPHESIANS 1:15–2:10

R
REFLECT
on your life

1 What is the most unique gift you've ever received?

_____

_____

_____

2 How do you determine what kind of gift to give to someone?

_____

_____

_____

R
READ
the passage

Read Ephesians 1:15–2:10, the chart "Our Lives Before and After Christ," and the following notes:

❏ 1:16, 17   ❏ 1:20-22   ❏ 1:22, 23   ❏ 2:3   ❏ 2:4, 5   ❏ 2:8, 9   ❏ 2:8-10

3 What gifts does God give believers to help them grow spiritually (1:17-18)?

_____

_____

_____

4 What does it mean to be dead because of your sins (2:1)?

_____

_____

_____

5 What does it mean to have been given life when Christ was raised from the dead (2:5)?

_____

_____

_____

_____

6 "God saved you by his grace when you believed" (2:8). What does this mean?

_____

_____

_____

_____

7 Rewrite Ephesians 2:8-9 in your own words.

_____

_____

_____

_____

_____

8 Given its awful consequences, why don't people take sin more seriously?

_____

_____

REALIZE
the principle

_____

_____

_____

Gifts, by definition, are free. They are given, not earned, and they should be accepted with gratitude. But sometimes gifts make us feel awkward or embarrassed because of the giver or the nature of the gift. We'd much rather earn what we are given or pay our own way. Salvation is a gift from God. Many people find that truth unsettling—it feels better to think that somehow we deserve what we get. But the fact is that while we were dead in our sins, God chose us—we did not choose him (1:11). He saved us by his grace. And even our faith to believe is a gift from God (2:8). Salvation and faith could only be gifts from God—we could never do enough to earn them. And without them, we'd be lost forever. Thank God for his grace and his gifts!

9 How do self-reliance and individualism make it difficult for us to accept God's free gift of salvation?

_____

_____

_____

_____

_____

10 Why do people today seldom talk about sin?

RESPOND
to the message

_____

_____

_____

_____

11 Review the chart "Our Lives Before and After Christ" and identify some concrete differences faith in Christ has made in your life. What were you like before you became a Christian?

_____

_____

_____

_____

_____

12 How should people respond to the fact that salvation is by grace alone?

_____

_____

_____

_____

13 What difference should this truth make in individuals' lives?

_____

_____

_____

_____

14 What can you do to demonstrate your gratitude to God for his gift of eternal life?

RESOLVE
to take action

_____

_____

_____

_____

_____

15 Out of gratitude for what Christ has done for you, how can you serve him this week? Think of something that you have never done before (take a walk in the woods to pray, share your faith with a close friend, help with worship at your church) that can creatively express your thankfulness.

_____

_____

_____

A Ephesians 2:3 speaks of the "inclinations of our sinful nature." What evidence of sin can you see in the world? in your life?

MORE
for studying
other themes
in this section

B What is Satan like, and how does he influence us? In what ways are Christians affected by Satan? What can we do to oppose the devil? How can we withstand his attacks?

C Christ is the head of the church, his body. What does this image suggest to you concerning the nature and function of the church? What part are you in the body of Christ?

LESSON 9
TEARING DOWN THE WALLS
EPHESIANS 2:11–3:21

REFLECT
on your life

1 What kinds of barriers separate people in our society? How can social barriers be removed?

_____

_____

_____

_____

_____

_____

READ
the passage

Read Ephesians 2:11–3:21 and the following notes:

❑ 2:11-13   ❑ 2:11-16   ❑ 2:14ff   ❑ 2:14-22   ❑ 2:19-22   ❑ 3:5, 6   ❑ 3:7
❑ 3:14, 15   ❑ 3:17-19

2 What wall divided us from God? How did Christ remove it?

_____

_____

_____

_____

_____

3 What does *reconciled* mean in 2:16?

_____

_____

_____

_____

4 Why does everyone need to be reconciled to God? How can this happen?

_____

_____

_____

_____

_____

5 How can people be reconciled to each other?

_____

_____

_____

_____

6 Given God's willingness to accept us into his family, how should this affect our relationships with other believers? with unbelievers?

REALIZE
the principle

_____

_____

_____

_____

_____

Although no one wants to admit it, all of us harbor prejudices—we find it difficult to accept certain kinds of people. So we cut ourselves off from them. But Christ came to reconcile us to God and to each other. The church isn't a social club where only those of similar interests, personality, and social standing are found. It is God's one, united family. Through Christ, God has torn down every wall that might separate us from him or from each other.

7 In what ways can it be costly to try to bring people together?

_____

_____

_____

_____

_____

8 What benefits and privileges come with being reconciled to God?

_____

_____

_____

_____

_____

9 What groups of people may find it difficult to be accepted in your church? How could you make them feel more comfortable and accepted?

_____

_____

_____

_____

_____

10 Why do Christians sometimes make certain people feel that they are not welcome in the church?

_____

_____

_____

_____

11 Who is an outsider at your church? What could you do to help that person experience God's reconciling love?

_____

_____

_____

12 What first step toward that person could you take this week?

_____

_____

_____

_____

A What do the terms *uncircumcised* and *circumcision* refer to (2:11)? Who would be in those groups in your church?

MORE
for studying
other themes
in this section

B How are we "built on the foundation of the apostles and the prophets" (2:20)? How does this relate to your church?

C How is the body of Christ like the temple (2:21-22)? How does God live in this dwelling?

D What special revelation was given to Paul in order to help him understand God's plan more fully? How does God reveal his will to us?

E Why does Paul refer to God's plan as mysterious (3:2-13)? To whom is God's plan still mysterious? Who needs to know what this mystery is all about? How can you tell them?

F How could Paul's suffering encourage the Ephesian believers (3:13)? How can our suffering help others? How can it glorify Christ?

LESSON 10
UNITED WE STAND
EPHESIANS 4:1-16

REFLECT
on your life

1 Think of a time when you were part of a team or group that was really "together." What contributed to that spirit of unity?

like Mindedness
a common goal

2 Why do people sometimes want to ruin the unity that others experience?

Jealousy, selfishness
Power

READ
the passage

Read Ephesians 4:1-16 and the following notes:

❑ 4:1, 2 ❑ 4:1-6 ❑ 4:3 ❑ 4:4-7 ❑ 4:11, 12 ❑ 4:12, 13 ❑ 4:14-16
❑ 4:15, 16

3 Why is unity important for the church?

we are to reflect Christ
in our communities + the world

4 Why is diversity important for the church?

each of us have such different gifts

5 In what ways can diversity conflict with unity?

When we don't work together & instead work against one another.

6 How should these two work together?

Vs 1-3 By being humble, gentle, patient w/ each other

keep united in the Spirit

7 What can believers do to keep themselves "united in the Spirit" (4:3)?

Prayer
Bible study
be willing to be led & do our part to keep the peace.

REALIZE
the principle

The body of Christ is much more than a collection of individual believers assembling at a convenient time and place for worship, prayer, and study. It is an interdependent body unified through our common faith in Christ. In God's marvelous wisdom, he has created and gifted each believer uniquely, so that we might complement each other in the work of building his Kingdom. While no local congregation can be perfectly harmonious this side of heaven, we should still look for ways to build one another up. We should avoid unnecessary dissension, disagreement, or conflict.

8 When is conflict needed and important in a church?

False Teaching

① Listen ② deliberate ③ make a
joint decision + find compromise

9 What are some signs of spiritual immaturity? How does it cause division and disunity in the body of Christ?

gossip
Having to have your own way.

10 Why do so many believers seem disinterested in attaining spiritual maturity?

Content where they are at.

Have salvation + don't want to grow

R
RESPOND
to the message

11 What actions and attitudes undermine unity within the church?

gossip
superiority
laziness

12 What actions should be taken by the members of your church to promote unity?

think before you speak
get involved
invite others to get involved.

13 What can be done to promote unity among churches in your denomination?

_____

_____

_____

14 What can be done to promote unity among churches in your town? Why are different congregations so hesitant to cooperate to attain common goals?

_____

_____

_____

_____

15 What are some ways that people can unknowingly or unintentionally foster dissension in a church? How can they best be made aware of their error?

_____

_____

_____

_____

16 What small step could you take to further the spirit of unity within your church? What are you doing that you should stop?

_____ *greet newcomers* _____

_____

_____

_____

RESOLVE
to take action

A Why does Paul refer to himself as a "prisoner for serving the Lord" (4:1)? In what ways are you Christ's prisoner?

B What "calling" (4:1) have believers received? What does it mean to "lead a life worthy of your calling" (4:1)?

C Ephesians 4:11-13 focuses on leadership gifts. What other spiritual gifts have been given to believers? What can your church do to identify spiritual gifts in the church?

D Why has God given the church various leadership roles? What are these roles? Are there any leadership roles that you could fill?

MORE
for studying
other themes
in this section

July 18, 2014

LESSON 11
LIVING IN THE LIGHT
EPHESIANS 4:17–5:20

REFLECT
on your life

1 List all the sources of light you can think of.

_the sun, electricity, fire
The Holy Spirit_

2 What are some of the uses we have for light?

READ
the passage

Read Ephesians 4:17–5:20 and the following notes:

❐ 4:17   ❐ 4:17-24   ❐ 4:28-32   ❐ 5:4   ❐ 5:5-7   ❐ 5:8   ❐ 5:10-14   ❐ 5:15, 16
❐ 5:18

3 List all of the examples of living in darkness that you see in 4:17–5:20.

_deceit, uncontrolled anger,
immorality, greed, obscenity,
telling lies, stealing._

4 Sum up what it means to live in the light.

_Be careful how you live
live in the Holy Spirits power.
Immerse yourself in His Word
Guard one heart + one minds
Be thankful._

5 What does it mean to "imitate God" (5:1)?

_____

_____

_____

_____

Living as children of light is quite a challenge! Unfortunately, we seldom live up to the high standard that God has set for us. While this should make us more thankful for God's forgiveness, it should also strengthen our desire to do what he wants. To live as children of light, we must let the light of the Spirit penetrate every corner of our lives. Then we should allow this light to illuminate the path that God wants us to follow. And finally, we should allow God's light to shine through us to show the way to others. It's time to leave the darkness behind.

6 Ideally, how should we respond when we become aware of sin in our lives? What is our natural response?

Confess it instead of excuse it,
deny it or blame others.

① recognize ② repent

true, helpful, inspiring, necessary, kind —
THINK

7 Paul wrote this letter to Christians. Why do believers want to continue walking in the darkness? What can churches do to help people walk in the light?

_____

_____

_____

_____

8 Describe a recent conversation you have had in which someone mentioned that your life was different. What can individual believers do to better shine as Christ's light in the world?

_____

_____

_____

_____

_____

9 What changes has God made in your life recently? Are you finding these easy or difficult to accept?

_____

_____

_____

_____

_____

10 Why do we resist the changes that God wants to make in our lives?

_____

_____

_____

_____

_____

RESOLVE
to take action

11 What are some of the areas of your life that you would rather keep hidden from the light of the Spirit?

_____

_____

_____

_____

_____

12 What one area will you make a matter of prayer? Ask God for the courage to open this area to the counsel and guidance of his Holy Spirit.

_____

_____

_____

_____

MORE
for studying
other themes
in this section

A How does a hardened heart contribute to living in the darkness? What can you do to keep your heart open to God's work in your life?

B What does it mean to "throw off your old sinful nature" and "put on your new nature" (4:22-24)?

C What is meant by the phrase "created to be like God" (4:24)? In what ways could this be interpreted wrongly?

D In what ways does anger give a "foothold to the devil" (4:27)? How can a person be angry and not sin? What makes you angry?

E What does it mean to "bring sorrow" to the Holy Spirit (4:30)? How do we keep from doing this?

F How is greed a form of idolatry? What other sins are also idolatry?

G What is the difference between forgiving sin and overlooking sin?

H Why aren't we *completely* changed when we accept Christ?

① good conscience

② blameless conscience (comes thru obedience)

③ clear conscience — without regret

④ weak conscience — not as mature

⑤ defiled conscience — begins to sin — testimony is destroyed

⑥ evil conscience — continually in sin

⑦ seared conscience — hardened — no feeling

LESSON 12
LOVING SUBMISSION
EPHESIANS 5:21–6:9

R
REFLECT
on your life

1 When is it easy to submit to authorities gladly and cheerfully?

when you agree w/ them.
when they're nice to you.

2 In what situations do you find it difficult to submit to others?

R
READ
the passage

Read Ephesians 5:21–6:9 and the following notes:

❒ 5:21, 22 ❒ 5:22-24 ❒ 5:22-28 ❒ 5:25ff ❒ 5:25-30 ❒ 6:1, 2 ❒ 6:1-4
❒ 6:5 ❒ 6:6-8

3 What guidelines does Paul give for wives and husbands?

4 What guidelines does Paul give for children and parents?

children are to honor their parents for life but parents are not to exasperate their children.

5 What guidelines does Paul give for slaves and masters?

Serve their master as unto the Lord w/ deep respect + fear. Please them + work enthusiastically

6 What role does mutual submission play in these relationships (5:21)?

Submission need to be done out of reverence for Christ –

7 What kind of submission should Christians display or exercise?

Mutual Submission – but no one is to be a doormat to another

REALIZE
the principle

Submission is a difficult subject for some people to discuss. And those who live in a democratic nation can tend to take the subject lightly. But Paul states that in the church all Christians should "submit to one another out of reverence for Christ" (5:21). In fact, when we have difficulty submitting to others, it may be because we refuse to submit to Christ. But Christian submission is different from a mere compliance with authority. Loving submission cannot be commanded by the one with the power in a relationship. It can only be given to another as a loving response. Let your submission to others in the church, at your job, and in your family be of the highest quality that you can offer each day.

8 How does the Bible's view of submission in relationships run counter to the world's view?

Society views submission as "weakness".

9 Why is the topic of submission often ignored or treated lightly in many churches?

very controversial

10 Views on submission in marriage differ. Some would emphasize the wife's submission to the husband (5:22), and others would emphasize mutual submission (5:21). What is your view on how submission ought to work in marriage?

_____

_____

_____

11 Why is submission so important in parent–child relationships? How does a parent teach a child to submit?

_____

_____

_____

_____

12 When is a person free from submitting to his or her parents? What is the difference between honoring your parents and submitting to them?

_____

_____

_____

_____

_____

13 To what degree should we submit to our supervisors and others at work? Where should we draw the line?

_____

_____

_____

_____

_____

14 Why is submitting to others usually very difficult? Why is it difficult even in the church?

_____

_____

_____

_____

15 How can your submission help bring others to Christ?

_____

_____

_____

16 Identify a relationship in which you need to be more loving as you exercise authority over someone. What can you do to meet this person's needs?

RESOLVE
to take action

_____

_____

_____

_____

_____

17 Identify a relationship in which you need to be more submissive to someone else. What can you do to submit more completely to that person's authority?

_____

_____

_____

_____

A What do the verses on husband-and-wife relationships teach us about the relationship between Christ and the church?

MORE
for studying
other themes
in this section

B What is the mystery mentioned in 5:31-32? In what ways does marriage mirror Christ's relationship with the church? How does your marriage illustrate that relationship?

C How does honoring parents lead to the fulfillment of the promise in 6:2-3? What can you do to more completely honor your parents?

D What should be some of the characteristics of headship in relationships? Where do you tend to fall short in the way that you handle authority?

LESSON 13
READY FOR BATTLE
EPHESIANS 6:10-24

REFLECT
on your life

1 What equipment and weapons does a modern soldier need for battle?

_____

_____

_____

2 What equipment and weapons did a knight on horseback use in battle?

_____

_____

3 What equipment and weapons did a Roman foot soldier use in battle?

_____

_____

_____

READ
the passage

Read Ephesians 6:10-24, the chart "God's Armor for Us," and the following notes:

❏ 6:10-17   ❏ 6:12   ❏ 6:18   ❏ 6:19, 20   ❏ 6:24

4 Why do Christians need the armor of God? Why would a Christian not want to put on all of God's armor (6:11)?

_____

_____

_____

_____

5 Which pieces of armor are defensive? Which ones are offensive?

_____

_____

_____

6 What is the role of courage (6:19-20)?

_____

_____

_____

7 Why do most Christians tend to take lightly our struggle against the spiritual forces of evil?

_____

_____

_____

_____

REALIZE
the principle

People tend to joke about the devil, but we must be careful not to underestimate our adversary. He is smarter and more powerful than we are and much more evil than we could ever imagine. That's why we must take precautions to protect and arm ourselves for battle. God has given us every piece of equipment we need, not only to protect ourselves, but to win! Put on your armor, sound the battle cry, and fight valiantly in the war that God has already assured us that we will win.

8 Why is it important for all believers to prepare for spiritual battle?

_____

_____

_____

9 In what ways can the church help its people to prepare?

_____

_____

_____

_____

_____

R
RESPOND
to the message

10 If our spiritual struggle were compared to a conventional war, where would you see yourself at this time: in the heat of the battle, at the front lines, with the reinforcements, mapping out strategy, helping with the supply lines, back at the base, in training, at boot camp, on leave, AWOL?

_____

_____

_____

11 Review the chart "God's Armor for Us." In what ways can each piece be helpful to you in your struggle against sin?

	Parallel to my life	*How can I use it?*
Belt of truth	_____	_____
	_____	_____
Body armor of God's righteousness	_____	_____
	_____	_____
Shoes of peace	_____	_____
	_____	_____
Shield of faith	_____	_____
	_____	_____
Helmet of salvation	_____	_____
	_____	_____
Sword of the Spirit	_____	_____
	_____	_____

12 Which of the above have you used the most? Which have you left unfastened or unused?

_____

_____

_____

13 Why is prayer important? How satisfied are you with your prayer life?

_____

_____

_____

_____

14 Churches are not immune to the attacks of Satan. What can churches do to improve their battle preparedness as a congregation?

_____

_____

_____

15 What can we do to encourage other believers and churches in their spiritual battles?

_____

_____

_____

16 Where is your spiritual armor weak? How might Satan take advantage of this?

_____

_____

_____

_____

_____

RESOLVE
to take action

17 What is the most important step that you can take right now to make yourself a better equipped and more effective soldier for spiritual battle?

_____

_____

_____

A What is the "time of evil" (6:13)? How will we know it has come, and what should we do when it does?

B What was the unique role of messengers like Tychicus (6:21) in the early church? How is this role fulfilled in the church today?

C Why was Paul's use of the battle and armor analogy highly appropriate for those to whom this letter was addressed? What could be another analogy for today?

MORE
for studying
other themes
in this section

Take Your Bible Study to the Next Level

The **Life Application Study Bible** helps you apply truths in God's Word to everyday life. It's packed with nearly 10,000 notes and features that make it today's #1–selling study Bible.

Life Application Notes: Thousands of Life Application notes help explain God's Word and challenge you to apply the truth of Scripture to your life.

Personality Profiles: You can benefit from the life experiences of over a hundred Bible figures.

Book Introductions: These provide vital statistics, an overview, and a timeline to help you quickly understand the message of each book.

Maps: Over 200 maps next to the Bible text highlight important Bible places and events.

Christian Worker's Resource: Enhance your ministry effectiveness with this practical supplement.

Charts: Over 260 charts help explain difficult concepts and relationships.

Harmony of the Gospels: Using a unique numbering system, the events from all four Gospels are harmonized into one chronological account.

Daily Reading Plan: This reading plan is your guide to reading through the entire Bible in one unforgettable year.

Topical Index: A master index provides instant access to Bible passages and features that address the topics on your mind.

Dictionary/Concordance: With entries for many of the important words in the Bible, this is an excellent starting place for studying the Bible text.

Available in the New Living Translation, New International Version, King James Version, and New King James Version. Take an interactive tour of the *Life Application Study Bible* at
www.NewLivingTranslation.com/LASB

CP0271

Prayer Request

7/15 ① Misty's Mom - dying of cirrhosis -
        home on Hospice
     strength for family - Dad, brother + her
   ② Heather - child care
   ③ Angie - job
   ④ Nicole - pregnant by rape -
        changes mind re: abortion
   ⑤ Illuminate / Legacy series
        ministry
   ⑥ God's direction for each of us.